T0273871

Praise for
Wealth is Women's Work

"The percentage of female financial planners has stalled out in recent years, but Peggy Ruhlin is here to say that needs to change. In this inspiring book, she discusses how women's skills, especially their empathy and practicality, make them ideally suited to careers in financial planning and wealth management. Chock-full of real-life stories drawn from Peggy's own career, *Wealth is Women's Work* makes a compelling case for the difference that financial planners can make in their clients' lives. The book also serves as an invaluable how-to guide for women who are considering a career in financial planning."

Christine Benz
Director of personal finance and retirement planning, Morningstar

"*Wealth is Women's Work* showcases the impact that visionary women like Peggy Ruhlin have made on the financial advice industry. From learning why financial planning is such an impactful career for women to illustrating the why and how to begin your journey in this inspirational profession, this book is a must-read for women at any stage of their career path. Peggy explains what so many of us in this profession already know: if you want to transform people's lives for the better, become a Certified Financial Planner."

Kate Healy
Managing director, Center for Financial Planning

"Peggy Ruhlin, a legend in the financial planning industry as a top female advisor and firm owner, has created a must-read book for any woman curious about a career in wealth management. She effectively addresses the many misconceptions that exist and shows how this noble career is one that focuses on assisting those preparing for an effective retirement. So many women think financial planning is all about the numbers, when in reality so much is about communication, listening, and learning—skill sets women tend to excel in."

Suzanne Siracuse
CEO, Suzanne Siracuse Consulting Services LLC

WEALTH
is Women's Work

WEALTH
is Women's Work

*How women can make
a long-term impact with a career
in wealth management*

Peggy Ruhlin

CPA/PFS, CFP®

Advantage | Books

Copyright © 2022 by Peggy Ruhlin.

All rights reserved. No part of this book may be used or reproduced in any manner whatsoever without prior written consent of the author, except as provided by the United States of America copyright law.

Published by Advantage, Charleston, South Carolina.
Member of Advantage Media.

ADVANTAGE is a registered trademark, and the Advantage colophon is a trademark of Advantage Media Group, Inc.

Printed in the United States of America.

10 9 8 7 6 5 4 3 2 1

ISBN: 978-1-64225-120-3 (Hardcover)
ISBN: 978-1-64225-437-2 (eBook)

LCCN: 2022920708

Cover design by Danna Steele.
Layout design by Wesley Strickland.

This publication is designed to provide accurate and authoritative information in regard to the subject matter covered. It is sold with the understanding that the publisher is not engaged in rendering legal, accounting, or other professional services. If legal advice or other expert assistance is required, the services of a competent professional person should be sought.

Advantage Media helps busy entrepreneurs, CEOs, and leaders write and publish a book to grow their business and become the authority in their field. Advantage authors comprise an exclusive community of industry professionals, idea-makers, and thought leaders. Do you have a book idea or manuscript for consideration? We would love to hear from you at **AdvantageMedia.com**.

For Jim Budros, CFP®,
for countless reasons

Contents

INTRODUCTION: 1
"How Are You Feeling?"

PART ONE 19

CHAPTER 1: 21
We *Need* More Women

CHAPTER 2: 37
"But I'm Not Good at Math"

CHAPTER 3: 47
"It's Boring"

CHAPTER 4: 55
"It's a Man's Field"

CHAPTER 5: 67
"I Don't Have the Right Skills"

CHAPTER 6: 75
"CFPs Only Work with Rich People"

PART TWO 81

CHAPTER 7: 83
CFP® Certification: The Standard of Excellence

CHAPTER 8: 99
Passing the Test

CHAPTER 9: 113
The Power of Internships

CHAPTER 10: 123
The Law of Attraction

CONCLUSION: 133
To My Fellow CPAs

TO MY INDUSTRY COLLEAGUES 135

ACKNOWLEDGMENTS 145

ABOUT THE AUTHOR 147

CONTACT 149

"How Are You Feeling?"

As WEALTH MANAGERS, the advisors at Budros, Ruhlin & Roe (BRR) spend a lot of their time talking to clients about investments—reviewing what to do, what *not* to do, why their investments performed the way they did, and how those same investments might perform in the future. Most of the time, these conversations are straightforward, as portfolios gain a little or even lose a little in any given quarter, but over longer periods of time generate positive returns.

That said, unexpected shifts can be unnerving for our clients. At those moments, client communication becomes more important than ever. They often need to be reassured that the market decline is not permanent, that their investment strategy still makes sense, and that they're not going to lose all their money! At these moments, we need to convince them that there is still good reason to trust us with their financial futures, because we understand both their immediate needs and the ongoing fluctuations of the market.

Some time ago, and after many quarters of steady gains, global stock markets took a sharp turn downward. The decline was steep enough to send our clients' portfolio returns into negative territory, and their quarterly investment reports were not going to be pretty. We knew we would be asked lots of questions and that some clients were going to be extremely upset, maybe even panicked.

Our chief investment officer (CIO) wanted to make sure our advisors were prepared to talk with their clients about the downturn, so he called a special meeting and put this to everyone: "Pretend I'm your client and I'm in the office for a meeting with you. I've just seen my investment report, and I know I've lost money. I want answers! What are you going to say to me?"

From body language alone, I could see that many of our advisors were on the defensive. I had a front-row seat to observe each associate's personal and professional comfort zone. That was when I started to notice something interesting.

One by one, the first few advisors took the floor. All of them happened to be men, all of them with eerily similar responses. Right away, they launched into a technical explanation of what happened.

"There was a stock market correction, because sentiment seemed to shift as concerns rose about a slowing global economy, tightening monetary policy, and continued political uncertainty."

"And the unresolved tariff dispute between the US and China ..."

"Oil prices have been extremely volatile and experienced steep declines ..."

"And there are mounting concerns about growing deficit and debt levels."

As I saw it, these associates wanted to demonstrate their knowledge and convince clients that they had a firm grasp of the situation. They knew their stuff! And that was true. They offered a very accurate, fact-based explanation for why the clients' returns were negative.

Then a woman took her turn. Her response was simple.

"Well, the first thing I would say to you is, 'How are you feeling? Are you OK?'" From there, this associate went on to explain that, after taking note of where her client was emotionally, she would decide on the best way to help them through.

She didn't come out of the gate swinging. Instead, she offered to sit back, listen, and evaluate the client's emotional well-being before saying anything else or sharing any facts.

I've always sensed that women operate differently than men, that we handle ourselves in a way that adds something unique to the workplace—something differently productive and often more creative. But after I sat and watched that display of those differences in action, I saw just how important the approach that's often described as "a woman's touch" could be, especially in moments of crisis.

The overall differences in the way the men and women in our office responded to the CIO's question was as bold as night and day. Both were correct. Still, there was something unusual about the way that woman approached the situation. When I sat back and placed myself in the client's shoes, I couldn't deny the fact that one of those methods could get us further, faster. The way the women approached handling the client revealed itself to me as an opportunity to really live our firm's core values of excellence, problem-solving, integrity, initiative, innovation, and, most important, collaboration.

Clients come to us looking for clear-cut explanations, but they also need to know that we care about their particular concerns.

Clients come to us looking for clear-cut explanations, but they also need to know that we care about their particular concerns. Think about it: if you just found out that you lost a significant amount of money in a short amount of time, what would you rather hear first from the firm that advised you? An inquiry into your well-being, or a clinical explanation of the many factors influencing the event?

The women could easily have begun their response with, "This happened because ..." but they recognized the need to lead with empathy.

"Hi, Jack and Jill. I understand your concern. I want to answer your questions, but first, let me make sure you're OK."

I'm not arguing that every client wants a pat on the back or a listening ear. But I will argue that everyone wants to believe that the people they trust with their money care about their well-being—in addition to their pocketbooks.

Nobody likes to lose money, no matter how much wealth they have already accumulated. Our exercise in light of the stock market tumbling forced me to witness just how much better the emotional overture of a particular approach—one that tends to be associated with and utilized more frequently by women—could go over. Establish or confirm the relationship first; deliver the technical follow-up later.

As the meeting went on, the theme remained consistent. Men leaned on logic; women uplifted with empathy. All were equally experienced. They all worked with clients on the same types of investments. However, that moment of stress brought out a very particular response. Listening, internalizing, and showing empathy was the approach taken by most of the women.

Let me say up front that the men in our office care about our clients just as much as the women do. They go out of their way to put their clients' needs first. And *everyone* has been trained to prioritize our relationship with the client when suggesting resolutions. Nevertheless, in that moment, I felt certain that what the financial planning industry needed more than anything was more women among its ranks.

And that's why I wrote this book. I want more women to choose wealth management for their careers. I want there to be more female financial advisors. I want to see more women leading financial advisory firms.

This book is aimed at two audiences: young women who are still in school (or even recent graduates) and who ought to know how wonderful the financial planning profession is and how rewarding a career in wealth management can be, and early-to-midcareer women who are just not satisfied in their present profession and who are wondering, "Is there something better out there for me?" Please read on.

It's Never Too Late

As the former chief executive officer (CEO) of BRR, I am proud to say that I've been recognized as one of our country's most distinguished women in wealth management. As a Certified Public Accountant (CPA) with a Personal Financial Specialist accreditation, and a Certified Financial Planner° certificant, I have had the pleasure of helping countless people reach their goals, both clients and colleagues. I've served on numerous boards and have been recognized in many professional spaces, but the one thing I love most is the fact that I can help create much-needed change in our profession: to attract and employ more women generally, and to promote more women into leadership roles.

I should admit up front that financial planning was not my very first career choice; I actually didn't find my way to this industry until a bit later in life. People aren't really shocked when I tell them that I didn't spend my childhood days dreaming of what it'd be like to one day help others manage their money. Like most people, I explored a few different paths before discovering the perfect career for me, doing my best to figure out what felt "right." For that reason, I make it a point to tell those who show an interest in this career path that it's never too late to try something new.

Before I became a financial planner, I had a career I thought I loved. Ironically enough, becoming a financial planner offered me all the benefits I enjoyed in my prior career—discipline, problem-solving, and building client relationships. Judging by all the happiness this profession has brought me over the last three decades and remembering the countless people I've worked with and all the lives I've had a hand in changing, part of me wishes that I would've made the career switch even sooner than I did—and I switched careers in my midthirties! Even though I want to share with you the joys of choosing a career in financial planning, my bigger message to you might be this: you can take charge of your life's journey. For me, that has meant finding ways to help others reach their highest potential. I might have achieved that in any number of ways. But the one I chose still seems the best of all the options for me.

I want to open up your options when it comes to choosing a career that might suit you well *and* give you the opportunity to live with a strong sense of purpose. It doesn't matter if you're a student, an enterprising millennial, or a curious empty-nester ready to remind the world of what she can do. I've written this book to tell you that no matter where you are in your career, or even if you're still thinking about a future career, you could choose to become a financial planner today.

Over the last thirty-five years, I've seen the wealth management business undergo many twists and turns, but in my opinion, there is no better time to consider this profession than right now. Every day, our work impacts the lives of countless people—not just those who work with us as clients, but the people who work for their companies and the people who benefit from their foundations, nonprofits, and partnerships all over the world.

In my opinion, there is no better time to consider this profession than right now.

That's why I've made a promise to invest my time and energy into helping other women become part of the financial planning profession. I want to invite more women into an industry that's very much in need of their services.

I want to undo the myths about financial planning careers, first and foremost the notion that these careers are not *for* women. In this book, I'll help you unwind some of the half-truths and misperceptions that hold back women's participation in the industry. For one, and as quiet as it's been kept, we financial planners don't spend our days up to our elbows in equations and calculations. To the contrary, the bulk of my workweek was spent hugging clients and shaking the hands of people who were thrilled to see evidence of just how much our firm has helped them. When I was not directly changing someone's life, my conversations were filled with thanks and appreciation from people who were so grateful that my company and I were able to help them secure their family's future for generations to come.

Like anyone engaged in meaningful work relationships, each day involved contact from clients, both present and past, who just wanted to share with me an update on how things were going for them. The "numbers" are just one part of our interaction—a significant but ultimately small one at that. My work allowed me to be a deeply engaged participant in other people's success and stability, and I want this book to be a call to action and a roadmap for you to do the same.

My Story

My journey began thirty-five years ago, when my then business partner suggested that we expand our services. I was working as a CPA, with mostly small business owners as my clients. Most of my workday was spent preparing financial statements and income tax returns. It was not lost on me that the work focused on what had already happened in a client's past. The favorite part of my job was meeting with clients to plan a future course of action to increase their cash flow or decrease their taxes. Several of those clients would mention to me that they'd also been working with a financial planner. In fact, in my role as their accountant, I occasionally attended meetings with those clients and their financial planners in order to review business results and tax projections. These clients were coming to me for accounting services, but they were depending on a financial planner to give them advice on retirement, estate planning, investing, and other important financial goals. Their relationship with me was necessary, but not the most central one when it came to charting their futures.

I grew frustrated that my only path for helping clients was to sort through the aftermath of their financial choices: *How much did you make? How much did you spend?*

The limit of what I could do to help my clients was to untangle the knotted web that was their income and expense statements or their tax return. That was when my partner made a brilliant suggestion. He mentioned the idea of having us take the necessary steps to become Certified Financial Planners too. Initially, I thought it would be interesting to consider but, to be quite honest, I didn't understand *exactly* what a financial planner did or what I'd have to do to earn the formal designation.

What I did understand was that without this added certification, my ties with my clients would always be rooted in generating an accurate account of their past lives. Given that helping clients move forward was my primary concern, I became curious about the difference I could make in their lives were I to add financial planning to the services I offered.

My partner and I had already invested quite a bit of time and effort into building relationships with our clients. From detailed conversations, we already knew their goals, and we knew what they did (or didn't do) to achieve them. The planning field may have been unfamiliar, but I was intrigued by the possibilities it could offer us. Most of all, I wanted to know that I could make a more significant difference in our clients' lives.

With that goal in mind, both my partner and I enrolled for a course of study with the College for Financial Planning and committed to doing whatever it took to become Certified Financial Planners.

I devoured as much information as I could. The more I learned, the more questions I had. That experience of renewed curiosity assured me that becoming a proactive force in my clients' planning efforts was the right path for me. Becoming a Certified Financial Planner would allow me to look into my clients' lives in real time so that I could help them make decisions that would positively influence their futures.

I signed up for a self-study program, from which I learned enough to pass all the required tests. It's true that I'd always been good at math. I come from a long line of number crunchers, actually. My father graduated from college with a degree in accounting. (I don't think he used it for more than a couple of years before he switched to a career in sales.) My grandfather, my father's father, was an accountant for the National Biscuit Company (Nabisco). Some may say accounting was in my genes, but I don't think that's what's made me a successful CFP. I honestly believe that, aside from my fondness for arithmetic and my accounting lineage, a big part of my success in this industry is due to me being a woman and my love of teaching others.

After I officially became a Certified Financial Planner, I started to offer financial planning as an adjunct to my accounting services. But it was really tough to find the time to actually *do* financial planning while I was so busy with my accounting and tax work. (Tax returns have deadlines; financial plans do not.) So when Jim Budros asked me to join him and practice financial planning, I jumped at the chance. This was one of the best choices I ever made in my life. I became a full-time financial planner, counseling and advising clients, and helping them plan their financial futures. I was finally doing what I had a passion for. (One side benefit was that I was able to go on vacation in March, something that was impossible as an accountant during tax season!) Our business grew—more clients, more employees. Jim and I took turns meeting with each client during quarterly planning sessions. Eventually, that meeting schedule became untenable, and we brought in a third partner, Dan Roe, to join us in counseling and advising our clients.

It's a truth that's become evident to me time and again. Whenever I sit down to reflect on the trajectory of my career, I can almost draw a line dividing it into two parts. In the beginning, I was a very hands-on, one-on-one, person-to-person advisor. I had clients with whom I met often and, truthfully, I loved every minute of that aspect of my career.

The second half of my career came about after our company expanded. Our business increased, and quickly. Days were consumed with client meetings, and those back-to-back sessions gave us very little spare time to invest back into the business we were building. It was the classic entrepreneur's dilemma: we were too busy working *in* the business to have time to work *on* the business.

Our lack of free time became such an issue that Jim, Dan, and I decided to devote a strategic planning session to resolving it. Around that time, we had begun having three-times-a-year offsite meetings with a business consultant / leadership coach, who was helping us learn to think long-term. He helped us realize that the only way for our firm to continue to succeed was for us to create a new position. As our organizational structure stood, we'd never carved out the space for someone to serve in a role like chief operating officer (COO), CEO, or some other executive leadership post. Not mincing words, our coach told us that we needed somebody to run the business. Until we charged someone with that specific task, we would keep running into the same growth issues we were facing at that moment.

Right away, we knew there were risks involved with such a change. Lessons learned from watching our peers hire a CEO or COO from the outside and then terminate their services after a year or two proved that organizational shifts like this had to be handled sensitively, and sensibly. Financial planning was a relatively new profession back then, so, in fact, most of those peer firms ended up spending more time trying to teach their new executive hires what a financial planner does rather than benefit from having a new CEO to manage company growth. In many cases, many of those new CEOs never really "got it," and, as a result, those businesses suffered.

After some discussion, one of my partners offered an objection: "It'll be over my dead body before I spend money paying somebody for two years, and they still just can't get it."

He was right.

We didn't have the money to spare or the time to waste. He suggested that one of the three of us had to take over the position;

he even offered to take on the role himself rather than make a bad outside hire. We were the ones who already understood what the business was about. Who'd be better suited for the job than one of us?

Our executive coach suggested that rather than make a hasty decision, we pause and take a minute to talk about which of us was best suited for that role. All the eyes in that room shifted toward me. Flattered, but slightly apprehensive, I agreed to take on the assignment. I didn't stop to think about it; I just agreed. Then I went home, slept on it, and talked it over with my husband. By the time I came back the next day, I had changed my mind.

Everyone groaned in disbelief.

"But why?"

It had seemed just the day before that we were all in agreement. Now there I was, less than twenty-four hours later, retracting my commitment.

Why did I change my mind? Because of fear.

I was scared that I couldn't do the job. I was afraid that I wouldn't succeed; I'd never been the CEO of a company before. But most of all, I was hesitant because part of me thought my partners wouldn't value my contributions to the business as much as theirs. As CEO, I wouldn't be working on the front lines with our clients anymore. I wondered if I could make the same impact from behind the scenes as I was making as an advisor.

My partners did their best to calm my concern. Confident in my ability to lead the business in the right direction, they urged me to reconsider. I agreed to reconsider but, this time, on my own terms.

During our brainstorming session, we had hung large pieces of blank paper around the room to record our ideas. I tore down one sheet of paper and wrote out a contract for my partners to sign. I promised to work in the executive role for two years, and two years only. After those two years were up, if I didn't want the position anymore, I would go back to being an advisor, no questions asked.

Those were my terms.

We all signed, and everyone agreed to the conditions. We brought aboard a fourth partner, John Schuman, to take my place in the client meeting rotation. Nearly twenty years went by, and I never exercised that escape clause.

Passion for my role in making lives more comfortable has carried me further than I ever would have expected. Both halves of my professional trajectory occurred within the same company in two very different, yet equally satisfying, roles. Over the years, I've been honored with awards and accreditations, two of which mark important professional milestones for me. I received the Alexandra Armstrong Award for Lifetime Achievement within the industry, a recognition marking the totality of my career—my contributions as a financial planner and a firm leader. That award helped me see that I'd really made a difference. The fact that the award is named for Alexandra Armstrong, one of the first women leaders of our profession and a personal hero to me, made it even more special.

Then there was the Charles Schwab Best-in-Business IMPACT™ Award, which was given to my firm in 2011. This award recognizes an independent investment advisor firm that has been in business for ten or more years and has elevated business management to new levels of excellence and achieved exceptional business results. Although I'd never give myself 100 percent of the credit for our success, I'd like to think that my management skills as CEO played a part in winning that award. Whereas the other award had helped me to see that I had made a difference in others' lives, this award helped me lay to rest that worry I'd experienced back when I was presented with the opportunity to lead our firm. I'd never had anything to fear. Not only was I a really good financial planner, but I'd also been a successful business executive.

Paying It Forward

Whenever I talk about my goal of inviting more women into the profession, I usually meet with at least some suspicion. Why do I believe there's a genuine need for more women CFPs?

The industry historically hasn't welcomed or encouraged the idea that women are more than capable of leaving a lasting impression. But I believe that the habits and skills that most women display are some of the very characteristics the wealth management profession desperately needs. Even today, industry reports and finance magazines might lead readers to believe that this is a "man's world," but I'm here to tell you that financial planning could very well become the next woman-dominated profession.

> *I believe that the habits and skills that most women display are some of the very characteristics the wealth management profession desperately needs.*

I've never been shy about calling out the financial world for its lack of opportunity for women, but now I'm glad to tell you those messages have started to be heard and acknowledged. Right now, not only are more firms creating initiatives exclusively for helping women launch successful financial planning careers, but they're making it easier than ever for women to break into the industry—even with little to no experience. And that means they're making it easier for successful women to reap the satisfactions that come from work-life balance, excellent pay, and participation in a respected field.

Each year, our firm hosts a client appreciation event, a party celebrating all those who've given us their trust by working with us. At a recent fall event, I was approached by a woman client who took a seat beside me. She had a big smile on her face as she put her arms around me and squeezed tight. Then she held my gaze and said, "I don't know how to thank you for how you changed my life!"

She went on to relate the story of her first meeting with me, and how I had recognized that she was less concerned about how to invest her new divorce settlement and more concerned about how she was going to balance her life and have enough time to be a newly divorced woman, a single parent to her three boys, and an effective elementary school teacher while still taking care of housecleaning, laundry, grocery shopping, and everything else. I had said to her, "I don't need to perform a financial analysis to tell you that you can afford to hire someone to clean your house. That's the first thing I recommend that you do with your money."

"Right then," she said, "I knew I was going to be OK and that I was in good hands. You actually listened to me, and you knew what I most needed to hear."

In recounting that conversation, she reminded me of one of the most important reasons for encouraging more women to become CFPs. A firm can have access to the best talent and resources, but the quality of that firm is measured in the concrete improvements it has made in others' lives. There was a particular way I had helped that client; I understood the specific set of circumstances with which she was faced at that moment in her life, and I had a simple solution to a problem that was easily fixed but seemed overwhelming to her. I was able to put her at ease in the midst of feelings of great doubt and being overwhelmed.

Now I get to use my role as chair and former CEO to teach the next generation of financial planners how to do what I did. I have the pleasure of helping them see the potential of a career in financial planning and getting them inspired to carry the torch.

After more than thirty years in the financial planning industry, I feel qualified enough to speak on what these next few decades have in store. I'm seizing this opportunity to open the door for women to explore a career in wealth management because, as I've seen too many times in the past, we are underrepresented on both sides of the desk.

Today we live in an era where pushback on gender divides has allowed women to climb to ranks once deemed too high to reach. Not that long ago, no one ever expected to see the day when women would hold high-ranking political offices, let alone run for president. In most fields, women have been carving out a path to success for years. Then there's the financial services industry. Just thirty-five years ago, I was told that only 25 percent of CFP certificants were women. Today, that number has *dropped* to 23 percent, despite the fact that, by 2030, it is projected that two-thirds of our country's assets will be controlled by women.[1]

If women are holding on to the nation's proverbial pocketbook, then why aren't we being represented in one of the areas that matters most?

Why aren't more women involved in wealth management?

I may not have a complete answer to that question today, but I do know what needs to happen in order to start changing the statistics, and the narrative, in favor of women. After understanding exactly how much authority I'm offered through my rank and role, I've committed my efforts to generating a guide, an official blueprint,

---

1 "Financial Facts for Women's History Month," The Quantum Group (March 13, 2017), https://thequantum.com/financial-facts-for-womens-history-month/.

regarding why and how women have the potential to be some of the most accomplished contributors to the financial planning industry.

My work with college students has helped me identify several commonly spread rumors that still scare young women away from a career in financial planning. In part one of this book, I will let you in on the truths behind those rumors. I'll offer answers to common questions like: Is it really a man's world? Do I have to pretend to be one of the guys? Do I need to be a number-crunching rocket scientist?

Then, in part two, you'll find a comprehensive step-by-step tutorial in everything you need to know to get your career as a financial planner off the ground.

It doesn't matter your background or your age; all you need to do is remember that financial planning is, first and foremost, a people business. If you think you're someone who's good with people, you'll likely be great as a CFP.

Together, we can modernize the financial planning industry and change the trajectory of your life in the process.

PART

1

CHAPTER 1:

We *Need* More Women

WHENEVER I BOOK A MASSAGE APPOINTMENT, the receptionist will ask, "Would you prefer a male or female therapist?" I am well aware that there are many women out there who want only a female masseuse. Similarly, many women prefer to have a female gynecologist. You might not expect that this tendency would hold strong when it comes to women's feelings about their financial planners, but the theme is the same. Somewhere between 55 and 70 percent of all women want to work with a female financial advisor.[2] That said, many of them haven't had the pleasure of doing so just yet.

When I first started out as a financial planner, women weren't involved much—if at all—in those conversations. The husband of a couple was almost always the primary breadwinner, and there was an unspoken, and uninterrogated, trust in the husband to do the right thing for the family. That was over thirty years ago. But *even today*, when married and long-term committed couples visit our firm, the

---

2   Theresa Gusman, "Now Is the Moment for Women Advisors and ESG Customization," *Greenmoney* (April 2021), https://greenmoney.com/now-is-the-moment-for-women-advisors-and-esg-customization/.

husband is more often than not the one in charge of the family's financial affairs and serves as the designated "lead negotiator" in decisions about money saving, spending, planning, and investment.

Women sat on the sidelines years ago, and to a surprising extent, they still stay out of the loop, often until it's too late to be heard.

Science has proven that women typically outlive their spouses, which means even if a wife spends the first twenty-five years of her marriage allowing her husband to handle the family's money, when he dies, she's going to need help making decisions that may be entirely new to her. Back in the day, some women wouldn't set foot in our offices until they were widowed and trying to salvage their family's estate. And still today, some women will accompany their husbands to meetings, only to indicate their disinterest in the decisions being made by reading on their phones or indulging some other obvious distraction.

At BRR, we have worked hard over the years to change this dynamic. As many as thirty years ago, we insisted that wives accompany their husbands to meetings and that they participate in making decisions that would affect the family finances.

Despite the efforts of firms like ours and the fact that household dynamics have changed considerably in the last few decades to involve more women in the financial planning process, it's still the case that women can't just walk into an office and find someone with whom they might instantly form a connection, someone who is "like them" even if only in physical appearance.

Imagine if you were making a massage appointment or selecting a new gynecologist only to discover that there were no (or very few) female practitioners available where you live. To those women who care about the gender of the person who is in a position to help them with these most personal matters, there will always be appreciation for the very fact of having the option to work with a woman instead of a man.

Beyond the need to see oneself reflected in a company's staff and in their leadership, it's even more important to enter a firm and sense that the people who work there have the emotional intelligence to recognize how important it is to invite women into the decision-making process. Making this important impression depends (at the very least initially, if not also later) on the actual presence of women on staff *and in leadership positions*.

Being able to click on a firm's website and see a woman featured on that company's website may be a relatively new phenomenon in the wealth management industry, but it is also an indicator of times to come. Small adjustments in the way our industry is constructed, marketed, and portrayed tell a story of a new day and age for financial planning. In this new narrative, one can find powerful women among the main characters.

Now Is the Time

If ever there was a time for women to establish their predominance in this industry, it's now and during the coming decades. The best firms in the business are searching for qualified women to join their companies.

They understand what a slew of studies, research groups, and publications have tracked and measured—all the amazing qualities women bring to the table. Take the work of Ragini Verma, for one, an associate professor at the Perelman School of Medicine

> *If ever there was a time for women to establish their predominance in this industry, it's now and during the coming decades.*

at the University of Pennsylvania, who identified that there are actual—and stark—neurological differences between men's and women's brains and even noted their complementarity. According to her findings, men's brains appear to be structured to take action, while women's brains tend to be better suited to carefully analyze a problem.[3] Cutting-edge firms understand that the best financial planning utilizes both of these skills in equal measure.

Let me clarify my argument in light of Verma's findings: I'm not engaging—and certainly not intending to fuel—a debate about which is the superior gender. I'm making a claim about what's best for the industry—and best for its clients. Clients want to work with advisors who look like they do. The business case is clear: when women are at the table, the discussion is richer, and the decision-making process is better.[4] It makes sense to imagine that clients would get better results (and be more satisfied) when they get the benefit of both male and female thought processes. I fully acknowledge and appreciate all the wonderful contributions made by the male partners and associates at BRR and in other firms. But I also know that including more women in financial planning careers would best serve our twenty-first-century clientele.

At the end of the day, this profession is about relationships. The relationships you have with your clients and the other advisors at your firm are absolutely central to your success. Everything you do, every decision you make, will always draw from and lean on those relationships.

---

3   "Sex Differences in the Structural Connectome of the Human Brain," *Proceedings of National Academy of Sciences* (December 2, 2013), https://www.sciencedaily.com/releases/2013/12/131202161935.htm.

4   Robin J. Ely and David A. Thomas, "Getting Serious About Diversity: Enough Already with the Business Case," *Harvard Business Review* (November–December 2020), https://hbr.org/2020/11/getting-serious-about-diversity-enough-already-with-the-business-case.

A successful financial planner must have the ability to build and maintain relationships with absolutely everyone. From current clients to prospective clients, to fellow associates at our firm, we come across a lot of different personality types—each one requiring a unique approach. Respect for the relational nature of our industry raises a different question: What is the basis of any great relationship?

If I were to ask a married couple, "What's been keeping your relationship together for so long?" I'm sure they'd give me answers that translate to *empathy, trust,* and *above-average listening skills.*

All of these are areas in which women often lead and excel. And they're just as important to financial planners as they are to newlyweds.

There's a lot on the line when a potential client meets with a financial planning firm. Before that client finds themselves walking down that aisle or, in this case, sitting at a desk with the contract from a wealth management firm in their hands, there are a few things that they need to be sure of.

First of all, they have to seriously believe within their heart of hearts that they can trust whomever they're getting involved with. They need to have faith in the firm, in the firm's leadership, and in their personal advisor. Then they must believe, without a shadow of a doubt, that all those people have their best interests in mind.

If you're a woman who's thinking about breaking into this industry, consider the extent to which the people in your life turn to you because of qualities like empathy, trust, and a listening ear. Are you someone who nurtures people and values honest and lasting relationships? When I say that financial planning is a people business, I mean that people want to feel valued. Clients come to us searching for someone who respects their opinion and who's willing to listen to, remember, and take seriously their needs.

Many of you may already believe that, in general, women are better listeners. You may be surprised to learn that there are research findings consistent across different groups, demographics, and settings to back up that hunch. In a 2015 study produced by Joe Folkman and Jack Zenger and published by *Forbes*, more than four thousand participants from all around the world were polled on their responses to an eight-point listening scale. Options were paired, and the respondents were asked to choose the statement that best described their approach. They were presented choices like these:

In a one-on-one discussion, I usually …

a) Take the time to understand others' issues and concerns. (84.2 percent response)

b) Provide others with a clear direction and purpose. (15.8 percent response)

To use coaching time most productively …

a) I take time to carefully understand the other person so that I can help them have personal insights. (56.4 percent response)

b) I translate my experience into practical, logical advice that helps people become more successful. (43.6 percent)

The study also conducted a 360 assessment featuring items designed to measure the participants' listening ability "as perceived by managers, peers, direct reports, and others associated with each respondent."[5]

Results showed that most people in business are reasonably decent listeners. However, when researchers took a closer look at specific groups within their pool of participants, there were some

---

5   Jack Zenger, "Age, Gender, and Ability to Listen: Who Listens Best?" *Forbes* (June 2015), https://www.forbes.com/sites/jackzenger/2015/06/11/age-gender-and-ability-to-listen-who-listens-best/#2906f93e9bf6.

significant differences. On a scale from –8 to +8, average results registered at about 5.13. When the results were divided by gender, women proved to be considerably better listeners than men. Women (5.28) even displayed a stronger natural preference for listening than men (4.94).

In a 2017 report published by *JAMA Internal Medicine*, three MDs from Boston evaluated the outcome of patients treated by male and female physicians.[6] After analyzing a 20 percent randomized sample of patients aged at least sixty-five years between 2011 and 2014, these doctors evaluated patterns between the physician's gender and thirty-day death or readmission rates. The results showed something remarkable: patients treated by women were less likely to die or return to the hospital once they'd been discharged. Mortality rates of patients with male physicians ranked at 11.49 percent while those patients with women physicians averaged about 11.07 percent. Male doctors had a readmission rate of 15.57 percent while female doctors saw only a 15.02 percent return for their patients. The authors of the study proclaimed that "approximately 32,000 fewer patients would die if male physicians could achieve the same outcomes as female physicians every year." Though they did not definitively identify the reason for these differences, the doctors surmised that it was due to the gap between both genders' listening skills. I always say that choosing a financial advisor is as difficult and important as

Choosing a financial advisor is as difficult and important as choosing a doctor, a lawyer, or a surgeon.

6   Y. Tsugawa, A. B. Jena, J. F. Figueroa, E. J. Orav, D. M. Blumenthal, and A. K. Jha, "Comparison of Hospital Mortality and Readmission Rates for Medicare Patients Treated by Male vs Female Physicians," *JAMA Intern Med* (February 1, 2017), 177(2): 206–213, DOI: 10.1001/jamainternmed.2016.7875, PMID: 27992617, PMCID: PMC5558155.

choosing a doctor, a lawyer, or a surgeon. People search for professionals they feel will relate to them.

At BRR, we emphasize with our associates, both male and female, the importance of establishing a trusting relationship with everyone. We explain why it's so important for every interaction to reinforce the idea that *we understand our clients* and empathize with their individual situations. We constantly reinforce with our newer advisors that the key to their success is not to come across as the smartest guy or gal in the room but to be the best listener and the best counselor. We strive to be the firm that listens, and I take our success as evidence of the importance of that skill.

I see some amazingly talented men in our firm tap into their empathy, trustworthiness, and listening skills every single day. But in the twenty-first century, more women are in control of their family's finances than ever before, and when those women walk into a financial firm like ours, they're making it clear that they want to sit down and talk with someone who looks like them and might share some of their gender-based experiences.

Think about it: baby boomers—the largest living adult generation—are of retirement age or older. Given that women typically outlive their spouses, that means there is a growing population of older female clients searching for help, and they have begun to search for someone to advise them. They need someone they can trust to help them take charge of their lives in a particularly vulnerable phase. Then consider that younger women are waiting longer to get married and have children—circumstances that require them to be responsible for their own finances in ways that women in prior generations hadn't needed to prioritize. And younger generations have been redefining gender roles and responsibilities in ways that make women even more likely to be proactive when it comes to financial planning and related concerns. Those young women have good jobs and money already saved, and they know how to seek out the help they need as they plan for their futures.

Women want to work with other women and to be assured of that option by what they see the second they look at a website or walk through the doors into a firm's offices. More and more firms understand that if they're going to keep the client happy and keep that relationship strong, they have to be prepared to give the client what they ask for.

The Invisible Wife

I remember many years ago, a new widow reached out to us and became a client. Her husband had recently passed away and, by her own admission, she knew absolutely nothing about investments. She told me she didn't know the difference between a stock and bond and, now finding herself in a position to control her family's money, she was completely petrified of the entire ordeal. She felt comfortable being vulnerable with me. Woman to woman, we had a connection. I understood where she was coming from, and I knew what she needed from me. So we spent the next few months building a solid relationship. As time progressed, she learned from our discussions and developed a familiarity with investment terminology. Her portfolio grew, and one day she came into the office to share some amazing news. With a smile on her face—absolutely beaming from ear to ear—she said to me, "I went to a cocktail party the other night, and the chat turned to investments. I spoke up and talked about how my money was invested, and people actually listened to me! I never thought I would know enough to listen in on—let alone contribute to—those types of conversations."

The Invisible Wife is a concept that isn't limited to financial planning or financial services. And it's a concept that doesn't even hinge on a wife's choice to be invisible. Let me give you an example from my personal experience. Some time ago, I was in the market for a new car, and I asked my husband to tag along with me while I chose what I wanted. We visited the car dealership. I made my choice. And then my husband and I found a salesman to speak with. I sat in the chair directly across from the salesman at his desk. My husband grabbed a chair and sat off to the side, waiting for us to finalize the transaction. To my surprise, the salesman looked away from me and began a full-blown conversation with my husband, as if I wasn't even there, let alone sitting right across from him. Even when I spoke up to ask a question, he'd look at my husband and answer *him*. Before long, my husband got annoyed. He cut the man off and said something like, "Hey, look, she's the one buying the car. I have nothing to say about it. You should be talking to *her*."

Not only was the salesman embarrassed (I hope), but he lost a sale. I was not going to spend my money at an establishment that wouldn't even acknowledge my presence. We left, and I bought my car from another dealership instead—one that didn't struggle with Invisible Wife sales tactics.

I'm guessing you can recall a time when you, or someone close to you, was affected by the Invisible Wife—or Invisible Woman—syndrome in some way. As frustrating as it may be, it still continues to happen too often—especially in those environments and professions that have traditionally been male dominated. At BRR, we've trained our advisors to know better—they regularly engage in role-playing exercises like the one I mentioned at the very start of this book, and they are responsible for observing and learning from the way that senior advisors and mentors speak to clients of both genders.

Setting an explicit goal of isolating and correcting Invisible Wife treatment was one of the reasons that, early on, we made it a necessity that both husband and wife were invited together to the decision-making table. It took only a few client interactions with that requirement in place for us to understand that doing so made clients more likely to implement our recommendations and more satisfied with our services. Sometimes, we had our work cut out for us convincing husbands that we fully expected their wives to attend every meeting and that they should recognize the importance of ensuring that their wives understood how the couple's money was managed. Eventually, even those who dragged their heels at the start came to see that this was better for them overall.

And for wives like the ones I mentioned earlier—the ones who assumed they didn't need to participate or were not being invited to do more than be physically present in the room—we worked to make sure that they understood their role in the discussion. We made a point of inquiring about each woman's needs and answering her questions and concerns, and we even made sure to tie the couple's concerns together by helping each one hear the other's perspective and then helping them agree about the goals they were establishing for their families. And what was perhaps the most radical thing we did at the time (and still do, of course) is that we had both husband and wife complete separate Risk Tolerance Questionnaires, a foundational assessment upon which an investment portfolio is constructed. (Typically, just one spouse, the one who makes most of the financial decisions or the one who is most knowledgeable about investments, completes the questionnaire.) Spouses seldom agree on how much risk they're willing to take with their investments—all the more reason it's important that both have a say in what happens with their money.

Of course, our efforts haven't been exactly foolproof. But on the other hand, there have also been a number of husbands who are *proactive* about their wives' involvement in financial planning. Those men already recognize the central emphasis of the financial planning business on relationships. Some men come into the office and say, "I absolutely want my wife to have a relationship with a financial planner with whom she feels comfortable, so if something happens to me, she'll have someone she can turn to who she trusts." Then, too, there are those families in which the wife is in charge of the family's finances, as well as cases in which the husband is the one inclined to scroll through his phone during our meetings with the couple. Knowing that our industry serves so many different dynamics is all the more reason for us to be prepared for each one of them.

At the heart of that preparation lies the need to invite more women to take up positions of authority within the financial planning industry.

Creating Opportunity

A lot changes when you're working with a company that advocates for gender-based modifications in the workplace. Those companies know that clients want to talk with female associates, that firms need successful women on their staffs. And now, the need that they've recognized and championed is becoming more and more visible, even to those firms that have yet to take up an advocacy role for female clients, associates, and leadership.

I mentioned earlier that only 23 percent of Certified Financial Planner certificants are women. If you were to look at the industry as a whole, the numbers would be significantly less; women represent just 15 to 20 percent of all advisors.[7] I can't tell you how many times in my career—even in just the five years leading up to publication of this book—I've been to a conference or wealth management event and, at most, 10 percent of the attendees were women. I can still use my joke about how there's never a line for the ladies' room! And I can still step back and comment on how few women are chosen to be featured speakers and expert panelists at these industry events.

Stepping back for that fuller-picture view, I can also observe that women are in control of over $22 trillion in American personal wealth. That's more than 51 percent of the country's total wealth—or what the industry recognizes as a built-in market.[8] Clients are making their preferences clear, and everyone knows that successful businesses generate satisfied clients made happy by services that are designed around their requests.

Businesses need their women clients to walk through their doors and *want* to sit down with their associates. Firms need women to *want* to stick around long enough to consider their expert suggestions and then follow through on those recommendations. It's not enough for clients to feel good when they're sitting down with us; we need those clients to *benefit* from our recommendations and to continue to trust our judgment. They have to know that every aspect of what we offer, from the advisors we select to the specific steps we suggest in their personal plans, is designed for their long-term flourishing.

That's why we need more women and diversified teams that can appeal to every client's needs.

Firms across the nation that recognize this fact are clearing the path for you right now. Financial planning executives are putting

---

7   Steve Garmhausen, "Women Make Great Financial Advisors. So Why Aren't There More?" *Barron's Advisor* (June 7–8, 2019).

8   "51% of Personal Wealth in the U.S. Is Controlled by Women," *Wealthtrack* (June 28, 2019), https://wealthtrack.com/51-percent-of-personal-wealth-in-the-u-s-is-controlled-by-women/.

their heads together to figure out what they can do to invite more women into the workplace. They've seen the studies outlining how companies are more profitable when there is a larger population of women on staff. More important, they've read the reports on how profitability increases even more when more women hold significant leadership positions.

It may still be the case that only 11 percent of senior executives of the world's five hundred largest companies are women.[9] It may still be true that 37 percent of those companies have all-male leadership, and 21 percent have only a single woman on the board.[10] Even so, there is also plenty of evidence showing the extent to which this is a problem for those companies. The Peterson Institute for International Economics released a survey of 21,980 firms from ninety-one countries around the world. Those companies that had women at the C-suite level experienced considerable increases in their net margins.[11] Moreover, they acknowledged that "a profitable firm at which 30 percent of leaders are women could expect to add more than 1 percentage point to its net margin compared with an otherwise similar firm with no female leaders. By way of comparison, the typical profitable firm … had a net profit margin of 6.4 percent, so a 1 percentage point increase represents a 15 percent boost to profitability."

In keeping with my point about the need for more women in leadership roles within the wealth management field and elsewhere, Joe Carella, assistant dean at the University of Arizona, Eller College of Management, conducted a study of Fortune 500 companies that

---

9   "Gender Forward Pioneer Index: World's Most Reputable Companies Have More Women in Senior Management," *Weber Schandwick* (March 2016), https://www.webershandwick.com/news/gender-forward-pioneer-index-most-reputable-companies-have-more-senior-wome/.

10   Ibid.

11   "Is Gender Diversity Profitable? Evidence from a Global Survey," Marcus Noland (PIIE), Tyler Moran (PIIE), and Barbara Kotschwar (PIIE), Working Paper 16-3 (February 2016), https://piie.com/publications/working-papers/gender-diversity-profitable-evidence-global-survey.

proved that placing women in executive management roles allowed the companies to benefit from what the study called "innovation intensity." These companies were proven to be more productive and creative, averaging 20 percent more patents than businesses run solely by men.[12]

Women continue to be faced with the task of overcoming misconceptions about our capabilities. For quite some time now, we have been working to change outdated narratives about our limitations or about the "proper" environments in which some of our most highly developed skills might be demonstrated and appreciated.

More than ever, financial services companies are aware that they're missing out if they don't have us in the room and make us comfortable there. Executives see that their companies would be more successful if they hired and promoted more women. And given the number of firms like ours that have recognized and embraced this reality, women with an interest in financial planning careers no longer have to walk blindly through the door and feel their way around a firm to determine its suitability for them.

12 Janet Zaretsky, "Want to Get More Money and Respect?" *Forbes* (March 8, 2019), https://www.forbes.com/sites/ellevate/2019/03/08/want-to-get-more-money-and-respect/?sh=2f8264dc4607.

CHAPTER 2:

"But I'm Not Good at Math"

MATH IS PROBLEM-SOLVING in the purest sense—you take some known facts and use them to solve a puzzle. I happen to love solving puzzles and trying to guess "who did it" in a mystery novel or movie. I also happen to love math. But I know I'm not typical, even among the people who thrive in my industry.

Nevertheless, quite a few people continue to believe that the only way to be successful in my line of work is to have always loved and been good at math—to have been a finance major in college, for example, or to have received an MBA. Some of the people who possess great soft skills that are an important part of what it takes to become a successful financial planner are turned off by the thought of having to do a lot of math. I want to convince those people in particular that needing to be really good at math in order to excel in this field is a myth.

It's Not Really about Math

Crunching numbers is a relatively small part of financial planning. Our roles, as I've already explained, are far more focused on establishing, growing, and maintaining relationships than anything else. You'd be surprised by the number of financial planners—absolutely great financial planners—who didn't get straight As in calculus or even take a calculus class in high school or college. I can guarantee that if you were to walk into any firm, you wouldn't need to look too far before coming across an associate who came "this" close to flunking eighth-grade math. Given the range of math skills among financial planners, we need to abandon the question that's usually asked: *Why in the world would anyone even attempt to pursue a wealth management career if they struggled with math in school?* and replace it with a new one: *Why does the myth that financial planners must be good at math still persist?* Those advisors who know that math is not an essential skill for a financial planner have done the research, completed their apprenticeships, and experienced for themselves the day-to-day rhythm of the job. They know that, as financial planners, we work with real people with real needs. Most of all, they know for a fact that if math isn't really your "thing," that's not an obstacle to success.

Now it's one thing to not enjoy math or to have identified that it is not a strong suit among your many talents. But when it comes to adult women and their assessment of their math skills, there's an even tougher hurdle to overcome. You may well be aware that math anxiety has been demonstrated to be higher in females than in males, and although the actual performance differences among genders is small to nonexistent, many women have had anxiety about their capabilities in this subject area since their grade-school days.[13] To summarize the research, math anxiety seems to be higher in females than in males, although gender-related differences regarding math performance are small or nonexistent.

I can't offer to resolve the anxiety that many women feel when it comes to their self-perception about their math abilities. But I can encourage you not to let math anxiety stop you from experiencing the particular satisfaction that comes from helping others solidify their financial futures. Know, too, that you aren't alone in your hesitation. Great men like Thomas Edison, Charles Darwin, and Alexander Graham Bell all expressed their lack of love for mathematical equations.

Luckily, in the modern world, a financial planner isn't even directly responsible for the mathematical calculations that affect their clients' lives. Nowadays—and the longer I've been in the business, the truer it's become—computers take care of most of the math for us.

Having said all that, if you, like me, really enjoy math, I assure you that there is enough of it to make you happy!

Problem-solving really is the most important part of financial planning, but the problems are not mathematical ones. Math is simply a tool used to solve some of the problems, and the skills needed to do that are both trainable and coachable. If you enjoy figuring out the best route to take on a long drive, delight in hunting through eBay to nab a collectible, or take pleasure in scouring the internet to find that toy a child desperately wants, then you're already engaging in exactly the sort of problem-solving we are called on to do as financial planners.

---

13   Hanneke I. Van Mier et al., "Gender Differences Regarding the Impact of Math Anxiety on Arithmetic Performance in Second and Fourth Graders," *Frontiers in Psychology*, vol. 9 2690 (January 18, 2019), DOI: 10.3389/fpsyg.2018.02690.

What It's Really All About

At BRR we have a saying: "We can teach smart, motivated people to be technically proficient (including the number crunching that is actually required), but we can't teach them to be great counselors." For that reason, the number one trait we look for in a potential advisor is the ability to communicate well—both clearly and kindly—with clients. We can teach and coach our advisors about the best ways to communicate specific types of advice, but the overall aptitude, or at the very least a strong willingness, to be good communicators is paramount.

> *The number one trait we look for in a potential advisor is the ability to communicate well—both clearly and kindly—with clients.*

My strong advice to you is to not let the myth of needing to be good at math play any role in your decision-making process about whether a career as a financial planner is right for you. If you know math is not your strong suit, focus instead on how you'll have innumerable opportunities to utilize your emotional intelligence. The wealth management field needs people with an aptitude for empathy and an openness to creative problem-solving.

Bottom line: if you can add, subtract, multiply, and divide, you have all the math skills you need to be a financial planner.

My best sense of the persistent power of the math myth is that we've carried into the present what was once true in the past but is no longer the case. When I first got into the financial planning business, there wasn't any software available for completing long-term planning analyses or investment reviews. It's true that, back then, even these two tasks alone were painstakingly laborious and time consuming. We'd have to review calculations in Excel, using an HP 12C calculator, or even in our heads! The systems we depended on back then weren't exactly nimble, and they were anything but intuitive. More than that, the entire computing process was flat, with every task completed using a very black-and-white, linear approach. You'd look at the client's documents and say, "OK, they have $500,000 now. If they earn, on average, 8 percent per year, how much money are they going to have in thirty years?"

But that is no longer the case. First of all, modern financial planning analysis is much more complex than that! Nothing about money is ever black and white, returns aren't linear, and it's impossible to predict what's going to happen thirty years from now. These days, there are no giant spreadsheets to prepare and decipher. We have far more sophisticated computer tools, which means that we can present clients with a far more accurate representation of the different possibilities for their future finances. Nearly all firms use software that both simplifies the calculation process and reduces the error rate to a minimum.

If you are curious about some of the products we use, I would encourage you to look into financial planning programs like eMoney or MoneyGuidePro. These are two of the most popular software options—precisely because they were designed to eliminate an advisor's need to engage in complex mathematical calculations. Nowadays, the requirements are simple. Remember? Add, subtract, multiply, and divide. You do need to know the basics, but that's about it. If you can carry out those four operations, you can succeed in this field.

> *Add, subtract, multiply, and divide. You do need to know the basics, but that's about it.*

Given that we now rely on complex technology to complete these time-consuming and difficult tasks, it's even more the case that an advisor's job entails:

1. Helping the client determine their goals: When do they want to retire? Do they want to buy a vacation home? Do they want to pay for their children's college education, and to what extent?

2. Working with the client to formulate some basic assumptions: What will their income look like from now to retirement? How much will the vacation home cost? Might their children attend a state school or an Ivy League college?

3. Using professional knowledge to make assumptions about inflation rates, investment rates of returns, the client's probable life expectancy, and other details.

4. Using professional skill to interpret the results of the software's financial analysis and to solve any problems: If the client is not projected to have enough money to retire when they want, what can be done to fix that?

The computer software will do the number crunching. All you have to do is understand math well enough to be able to explain to a client that the computer analysis indicates they need to save $10,000 more per year for the next twenty years in order to meet their retirement goal.

The Truth: A Day in the Life of a Financial Planner

I invited a couple of the women advisors at my firm to share a glimpse into their schedules during an average week in the office. Here's what they agreed a four-day period might look like:

Day 1

- Review assumptions, prepare long-term planning projection using eMoney software, and formulate recommendations in preparation for client meeting

- Conduct phone call with client to touch base and review investment reports

- Prepare minutes from last week's client meetings

- Attend Financial Planning Committee (internal) meeting

- Meet with client to review long-term planning projection and recommendations

- Meet with team about "to-dos" and upcoming meetings

- Check and respond to emails and client texts

Day 2

- Prepare and review for client teleconference about disability insurance

- Attend New CRM (internal) meeting

- Meet with client

- Prepare for the next day's meetings

- Check and respond to emails and client texts

Day 3

- Meet with team about "to-dos" and upcoming client meetings

- Receive phone call from client: questions about cash needs for gifts to children and discussion about safe withdrawal rate

- Teleconference with client: disability insurance review/needs

- Prepare for the next day's meeting

- Conduct call with client: planning for travel out of state to meet with them

- Check and respond to emails and client texts

Day 4

- Prepare for next week's client meetings

- Teleconference with client: investment performance

- Prepare quarterly client investment reviews; enter trade recommendations in rebalancing software

- Check and respond to emails and client texts

There's work to be done that requires any advisor to exercise intelligence and analytic skills, but that work neither amounts to nor involves any strong mathematical capabilities.

CHAPTER 3:

"It's Boring"

WHENEVER I SPEAK at conferences or give presentations at colleges around the country, as soon as the floor is opened for questions, someone will stand up and challenge me: "But how can you tell us that financial planning is so great, when all you do is talk about investments?" or "Sitting in front of a computer every day analyzing investments seems painfully boring."

I've heard the refrain "It sounds so boring" so often that I had to step back and consider where this assumption could have come from. I know how fulfilling and engaging my time as a financial planner has been, and so I needed to understand exactly why I keep running into the idea—the conviction—among audience members that wealth management is such a drab and lifeless field.

I believe this myth is centered on a perception that financial planning involves nothing more than selecting investments for clients—and that the process of doing so is inherently uninteresting. But even if I were to consider movies or pop cultural references that make "selecting investments" look far more interesting than most people might believe, those cultural reference points also present an image that's a far cry from what financial planning actually entails. *The Wolf of Wall Street* or *Trading Places*, for example, is as much about financial planning as the Harry Potter movies are about a guy who makes ceramics. I remember being excited when the Netflix series *Ozark* premiered—the star, Jason Bateman, played the part of "financial planner" Marty Byrde! Intriguing as the show's story line was, I didn't see any financial planning going on, just investment-making (and money laundering). There just aren't any good or, for that matter, accurate portrayals of the industry circulating in contemporary culture.

On top of that, the investment portfolio may very well be an important part of a financial plan, but it is just *one* part! Planners not only have to manage their clients' investments, but they also have to monitor their clients' spending and debt, keep watch on client savings and retirement plan contributions, ensure that taxes are legally minimized and paid on time, advise on employee benefit packages, review estate plans and life insurance policies, and so much more. Again, part of the job does deal with investments, but a lot of the job does not.

Variety: The Spice of Life

When I was in grade school, there were basically two occupations a young woman could pursue—nursing or teaching. I always said that I wanted to be a teacher. I was one of those nerdy kids who, during summer vacations, would round up the younger ones and force them to sit in neatly arranged rows in my basement "classroom." I even had a blackboard for writing out the day's lessons. I taught whatever topics I could think of, all summer long (or for as long as they'd let me). By the time I got to college, there were more fields opening up to women, and my aspirations to become a teacher eventually fell by the wayside. That said, I do tend to think that a good portion of what I do today is a form of teaching. Teaching is, after all, a helping profession.

And just like a teacher might be called on to switch among subjects throughout the day, so, too, do financial planners switch between a variety of duties and responsibilities. It's that variety—the fact that we're absolutely not sitting behind our desks punching numbers into computer programs all day—that's one of the aspects of the job I find most appealing.

There's visiting and camaraderie: when we meet with clients, we're building mutual rapport and enjoying one another's company. There's teaching or helping to build our clients' skill sets by encouraging learning and sharing information and analysis. There's armchair psychology and life coaching: people have all sorts of emotional responses to conversations about money, and they often have surprising ideas and misunderstandings about their finances—some of which they've held unquestioningly since they were children listening in as their parents discussed the family's finances. And given that clients are asked to do nothing short of thinking carefully about their futures, they may make interesting discoveries about what they want for themselves along the way. For example, after many years of working with a client who was a successful dentist in Ohio, we finally helped him figure out that his real goals were to live in Colorado and to work as an EMT.

Besides the variety of roles you might take up to assist clients with their planning processes, you'll also find yourself spending a lot of time talking with all kinds of people doing all sorts of interesting things. You'll hear fascinating stories about their lives, learn about their different backgrounds, and entertain their dreams. And you'll find yourself responding to inquiries of all kinds: one person might call you to talk about an article they read that they don't understand; another will confess their fears or worries about current economic forecasts. Our clients depend on us to support them in a number of different ways and to use our intelligence and our problem-solving skills to advise them in whatever ways they need from us right then. Finally, given that relationships between advisors and clients are ongoing, you'll develop the sorts of relationships I mentioned in an earlier chapter—the kind of long-term bonds that come from being a trusted resource with intimate knowledge of your clients' lives. An advisor who has been building an ongoing relationship with a client over a matter of years has a different "gateway" into the client's attention and a great responsibility to honor that access with deep and caring professionalism.

There aren't any movies, TV shows, or even blogs about wealth managers seeing a couple walk into the office to review their financial plan because they're expecting their first child. Not much is recorded about the gratification that comes from helping that couple reevaluate their short- and long-term goals, and, a few months later, seeing their beautiful baby come with them to a meeting.

Financial planners have the privilege of being present for, and acting as a force for good during, life's biggest transitions.

Financial planners have the privilege of being present for, and acting as a force for good during, life's biggest transitions. We guide clients through planning for weddings, graduations, home purchases, promotions, vacations, new grandchildren, and so much more. Although many of those transitions are positive ones, we're just as much present to help clients through their most difficult times—divorces, deaths, and other big losses. And we bring clients through conflict—serving as mediators, especially when it comes to negotiations within couples when each person has very different opinions about spending and saving. Those dilemmas need to be addressed and worked through, and we are there in the room guiding those conversations in an attempt to find resolution.

It's my guess that if you were to sit down with almost any financial planner, they'd have several lifetimes' worth of interesting stories to share. Their focus may be on finances, but in drawing attention there, they will also have helped people through life-altering events and toward the achievement of satisfaction and even joy in reaching their goals.

Financial planners help people come to terms with what is the case and set goals for what could be. It's true that we're not trained therapists—nor do we ever pretend to be—but we do take courses on client communication, and we do participate in ongoing training and mentoring on using our best judgment when it comes to having productive client conversations. There's even a specific area of financial planning, sometimes referred to as life planning, in which the sorts of skills I've mentioned here come even more regularly into play. More than anything, our training and experience teaches us to be agile conversation partners and to adapt our actions to clients' needs—on any given day and under any given set of circumstances.

My colleague Andrea recently shared with me a conversation with one of her clients. The client called because she had just received a tax notice from the IRS and didn't know what it was about or what to do with it. About forty-five minutes later, the client and Andrea were still on the phone talking about any—and every—thing except taxes.

Andrea understood that the client's biggest issue at that moment wasn't the paper in her hands; it was the need to feel confident and supported right then and there. Rather than coldly get to the point, Andrea was patient and let the client express her broader concerns. Experience had taught Andrea that some people call because they just need to talk and that being a receptive listener is just one of the many roles she plays as an advisor.

This profession is a lot of things. We get to wear many hats, and during any given hour, we can't say for certain that we know which of those hats we'll be asked to wear. That makes for a fuller, and more fulfilling, work experience than many other finance careers. I've formed connections that transcend generations of family members. I've traveled to places I never thought I'd visit. This profession has allowed me to meet some very interesting, and even famous, people like former presidents Bill Clinton and George W. Bush, former chair of the Federal Reserve and secretary of the Treasury Janet Yellen, and former secretary of state Condoleezza Rice. I also got to introduce former British prime minister David Cameron at an industry conference. And I've met not one, not two, but three Nobel laureates in economics. Once, at a small conference, I had a lovely lunch with another Nobel Prize winner, William Sharpe, and was thrilled that I got to take a picture with him. Sometime later, I proudly showed off the photo to my then twentysomething daughter.

> *This career is not boring; I know that from experience.*

I asked her if she knew who he was, and she asked, curiously, "Is he in a rock band or something?" To me, meeting him was, in fact, like meeting a rock star.

This career is not boring; I know that from experience.

Clients watch us. They study us. They judge our capacity to offer them real help. It's no small task to convince them of our dependability and our worthiness of their trust. In every conversation, we're proving that we're committed to the promise we made to do our very best work on their behalf. Succeeding at that task is a feeling like no other. It's a personal business; that's one of the things I love most about it. That's also why I'm so passionate about making sure that other women know the truth about this profession and feel welcomed into it.

CHAPTER 4:

"It's a Man's Field"

THE IDEA THAT WEALTH MANAGEMENT is an industry strictly reserved for men has long passed its expiration date. You may not personally know any women who are financial planners, but that doesn't mean that we aren't here and successful.

That's not to say that visiting the websites of many of the industry's firms will show you we're here. There are, in other words, still a surprising number of firms that don't have a thriving cohort of female financial planners. What I do know from all my contacts and colleagues in the industry is that the men who end up working for those firms don't want to be in an environment that unfairly excludes their female counterparts. Nearly everyone involved wants to change the narrative—to make it more of a myth than a reality—that financial planning is a man's field.

As for the CEOs of those male-centric firms, I'm sure they have wives, daughters, sisters, and mothers who mean a lot to them. I'm sure, too, that as we continue to raise awareness of the elephant in the room, they would like nothing more than to be part of establishing a new social narrative, one that'll give the women in their lives a fairer shot.

What most if not all firms *do* currently have on their websites, to the advantage of any women thinking about becoming financial planners, is information about their diversity and inclusion initiatives. That means they're willing to invest in making sure that their new colleagues have all the support they need to stick around for the long haul.

And the dearth of women's faces on those websites? Maybe that's more a reflection of outdated sites themselves than it is of who you would actually see were you to walk into their offices. Though I recommend learning everything you can about any firm you might be interested in working for, I can warn you that the photos and bios on the "About Us" pages at some firms may represent only a small fraction of who's actually in the office. I know it may take a little longer for you to find snapshot bios of women advisors online, but the tide is changing, and the marketplace is driving firms that haven't yet changed toward opening their arms to more women. I'm not talking about the administrative assistants in the office. I'm talking about the slow but steady shift away from the imbalance of all-male advisors and all-female support staff.

My personal journey in this field isn't one I'd recommend to the faint of heart. At times, it felt like wealth management didn't just have a glass ceiling over it, but an iron ceiling on top of that! My point here is that having had that experience, I am able to see that today we are breaking through those ceilings for good.

Women for Women

As financial advisory firms continue to see the writing on the wall, they're recognizing the need to take decisive action. They know it's not enough simply to hire more women. They need the public to know about their commitment to seeing women succeed in an industry that all but left them behind for decades. These firms are acutely aware of the ultimatum they're being given: either hire, promote, and feature more women advisors or run the risk of losing the attention of the next generation of customers, both female *and* male. Those customers are advocates for inclusion and diversity. Those customers want to see themselves represented when they seek out the support of a financial planner.

> *Either hire, promote, and feature more women advisors or run the risk of losing the attention of the next generation of customers.*

But even given increasing customer demand, women have not been entering this industry at record speed. According to the CFP Board, as of 2020, there were 20,633 female Certified Financial Planners in the US—just 23.3 percent of all CFP certificants.

I pointed out in an earlier chapter that women are more clearly expressing a desire to work with other women. That insight is true for both clients and planners alike. If a woman client walks into a firm with no preference for working with a male or female advisor, but she doesn't see any women planners around, I believe that firm is still very likely to lose out on her business. She may begin with no preference but be put off by the invisibility of women in positions of power.

Likewise, if a talented woman planner sees that a firm does not have female clients or treats those clients less respectfully than their male counterparts, she may not wish to join the firm, or she may leave for another soon after coming on board. In both instances, the prospective client or planner could spark a domino effect, spreading word of how that firm is still working from an outdated patriarchal script. In no instance would that be a good thing.

The good news is that financial advisory firms nationwide are putting real effort into helping the wealth management space readily display that it is the inclusive environment we're all aiming for. As an insider, I can tell you that just about every financial advisory firm in the nation believes it is critical to hire more women. *There's never been a better time for women to find work as financial advisors.*

A Round of Applause

As the world of wealth management sheds the remnants of having been for so long a "man's world," our male counterparts have been stepping up to congratulate women who've proven successful at the work. More and more firms are nominating their hardest-working women advisors to *Forbes* magazine's annual list of "Top Women Wealth Advisors." In 2020, there were one thousand women listed! While the list is wirehouse-centric—with Merrill Lynch, J.P. Morgan, Morgan Stanley, and the other big firms heavily represented—there are several women from independent wealth management firms. If you look up the list, you'll find women like Debra Wetherby, who runs a $5.3 billion company (Wetherby Asset Management) in San Francisco, and Heather Locus, a wealth advisor at Balasa Dinverno Foltz in Chicago. What makes this *Forbes* list so special is the fact that it doesn't just look at the numbers. It examines the very thing I've been emphasizing in making the case for more women advisors, and that's the *client experience.*

The ranking system used to decide which advisors would be featured on the 2020 list didn't stop at the amount of assets under management. SHOOK® Research looked at more than the numbers; they used an algorithm that combines qualitive and quantitative data gathered through in-person interviews with the nominees and a summary of nominees' industry experience, including certain compliance factors, revenue, and assets being managed.

Former Duke swimming alumna Teri Conklin, one of the 2020 Top Advisors, describes her experience coming up through the ranks at a time when women were not as welcomed as today: "It was just a working environment with many men and there weren't a lot of me.... I just applied the same principles I had as a ... swimmer to work, and that's helped me more than worrying about when I'm not getting the best deal that the guy does."[14] Jane Rojas of Morgan Stanley in Tucson, Arizona, draws attention not only to the need for women advisors but to the need for non-white-identifying women in her 2019 interview with *Forbes*. She said then, "If you look at the average FA [financial advisor] today, he's fifty-eight years old, white, male. Only 15 percent of FAs out in the field are women. That needs to change because our client demographics and the communities we come from don't look like that."[15]

Jane's right. And she's not alone in her argument. In fact, women have been singing this song for so long it might be a surprise that we are finally seeing significant change. We have been changing the opinions of men in the industry and changing the public face of the

---

14   Jason Bisnof, "Top Women Advisors: Strategies for Volatility and Winning in a Male-Dominated Business," *Forbes* (April 2020), https://www.forbes.com/sites/jasonbisnoff/2020/04/21/top-women-advisors-strategies-for-volatility-and-winning-in-a-male-dominated-business/?sh=29ace0c15477.

15   Jonathan Ponciano, "Main Street to Wall Street: How This Advisor's Border-Town Upbringing Helped Build Her $500 Million Practice," *Forbes* (April 2019), https://www.forbes.com/sites/jonathanponciano/2019/04/30/this-main-street-advisor-has-the-wall-street-edge/?sh=77bdc8787d76.

industry; now it's up to us women to fill in the blanks, to bridge the gap between what is and what could be, and to balance out still-disproportionate figures by entering the field at greater rates than in the past.

I'm going to make a potentially unpopular argument, but I do so because I see that a door has opened, and I want to encourage women to take advantage of this tremendous opportunity to alter the trajectory of the field for good: I need you to believe in yourself, to let your curiosity about financial planning open new doors for you. I need you to know that those doors will open. At the very least, they'll open as they have for many women before you. At the very best, they'll open even wider to welcome you in. As of right now, I want you to focus on this new mantra: financial planning isn't a "man's world" anymore. We're on the threshold of creating a brand-new wealth management community.

If you're interested in wealth management, please believe me when I tell you that *now* is the time for submitting a résumé to your dream firm. Please believe me, too, when I tell you that self-defeating thoughts ("It's a man's world. They don't want *me*. I can't do this.") are right now only just that—self-defeating. If nothing else, remember that there are those who've come before you who have gone to great lengths to prove that men could learn a thing or two from the women who've earned a spot among them.

If you're interested in a wealth management career, also know this: a widely quoted anecdote from Sheryl Sandberg's *Lean In* (itself quoting an internal Hewlett-Packard report) tells that a man can see an opportunity that catches his eye, read through the job description only to find that he's, at best, 60 percent qualified for the role, and still apply. To the contrary, a woman can lack a mere 1 percent of the expectations described, and she'll talk herself out of applying. Men don't doubt themselves as often, or as much, as women doubt themselves, so the story goes.

Later studies have kind of debunked this "theory," but if you're one of those women who needs to work on building up your professional confidence, think of Jane Rojas and Teri Conklin and all the other women who've appeared on that *Forbes* list. Whenever you begin to doubt your abilities and your capacity to learn new things, think of all the women who battled social stigmas and patriarchal environments to arrive at the point in the field's history when you can be not just invited in but welcomed. Remember these women, and then think of the person who's out there somewhere waiting to be inspired by your story too.

Guts before Glory

Most ambitious people can't wait for the day that they get to "see their name in lights," the day when success and recognition within their professional communities gives them a sense that they can finally say "all that hard work was worthwhile." For most of us, in most careers, we have to earn our accolades. We begin with learning and deep study, and we follow that up with commitment to our work and a willingness to dig in when challenges arise.

Most careers, too, offer a clear path from training to success story. Let's take attorneys as an example. We know the typical path of a new law school grad is to enter a law firm as an associate working eighty hours a week for a senior partner. It's not exactly fun, and it's a tremendous amount of work. Some would even argue that it isn't fair. But that's the way things work in the legal field. New associates bust their behinds until someone higher up the hierarchy acknowledges that they've successfully paid their dues and earned a promotion.

Keep up that routine for a good seven years, and maybe you'll be invited to become a junior partner. On it goes from there.

As much like a form of "hazing" as this early part of the process sounds, it's also relatively straightforward. One step is intended to lead clearly to another, and both women and men make their way through the process to positions that indicate career success.

Wealth management is different in the sense that it's not always easy for women in particular to *see* the payoff of career progress in the field. By that I mean that it takes *a lot* of dedication to reach the level of those *Forbes* all-stars. In wealth management, there are many women who have reached top levels and had remarkable accomplishments, but they are often unseen or unacknowledged with titles and awards. It is still far too common that our shared picture of a financial advisor—the very picture reinforced by corporate marketing departments and advertising agencies—is the image of a white male in a suit. Charles Schwab appears on TV commercials during NFL games; people don't see the Peggy Ruhlins of the world.

While I am in no way trying to compare myself to the likes of Charles Schwab in terms of public recognition or business success, I am saying that it's hard for women—even very successful women—to feel recognized in this field. That's absolutely a product of the fact that women are still earning their place within the industry, much as they are more clearly being welcomed into it now. It's still difficult for a woman advisor to look around and be inspired by the work of another woman prominently on display.

> *It's hard for women—even very successful women—to feel recognized in this field.*

That said, we celebrate the publications that make a point of honoring the work of women in wealth management. In addition to that *Forbes* list, *Investment News* has a program called "Women to Watch." Each year, twenty women are chosen for this feature. "Women to Watch" is printed as its own separate publication and not just buried in the back pages of a standard edition. Similar to the women on *Forbes*'s list, each of the "Women to Watch" has a unique story of working her way to success in the wealth management field. There are young women, middle-aged women, and women from all races, creeds, and colors featured in that publication. So, if you know where to look, there *are* resources to which you can turn for inspiration. Additionally, not only is the "Women to Watch" list a resource for those women who may be considering a career in financial planning or are actively engaged in its early phases, but it's also a great reminder for the men—especially those in positions of power. It's an additional bit of proof that women are forces to be reckoned with in the field, and it lets any resistant male executives know that they're on notice when it comes to adding women to their teams.

Investment News started the "Women to Watch" project as recently as 2016. Each year since then, it has continued to raise the bar. In just a handful of years, the publication of the list has transitioned to being backed by a huge event held in New York each year where the industry comes together to celebrate the women honored in that year's edition. When I saw it for myself, I was flabbergasted by how many women were in attendance. The initial event had about one hundred attendees, but in a couple of years, it moved to a larger facility that could accommodate more than five hundred and has continued to grow from there. That's a tremendous evolution within a short period of time. Programs like this one stand as evidence of how quickly the situation is changing within the field. It's proof that the industry as a whole understands that it has to adapt to that change.

I don't think I would be wrong to assert that every major financial services firm in the United States now has some kind of women's outreach or gender diversity program. For example, Charles Schwab has the Women's Interactive Network at Schwab (WINS). Goldman Sachs announced in 2018 its goal of having 50 percent of its college campus recruits be women. Even small firms like BRR have implemented some sort of campaign designed to attract more women and create more outreach targeting them.

As someone who's lived through a time when this sort of effort was unheard of, let me say that it's always nice to see a company put its money where its mouth is. That's still a fine measurement of whether or not said company is just paying lip service or proving that it really wants to be at the forefront of change. It's a sign—just the sort of recognition we seek—letting us know that no matter how long the myths have been around and become part of our culture and our individualized assumptions, the time has come to write a new chapter.

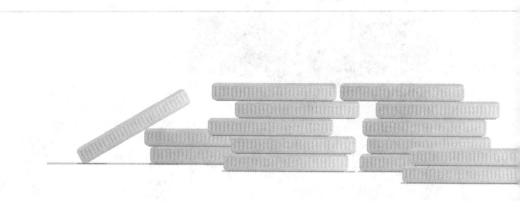

CHAPTER 5:

"I Don't Have the Right Skills"

"PEOPLE FEAR WHAT THEY DON'T KNOW," goes the saying, and I think it rings true when it comes to women's underestimation of their ability to be successful financial advisors. By now, I hope you've come to recognize that the field of financial planning encompasses so many different roles and responsibilities that it would be genuinely difficult for anyone to say they aren't skilled enough to do something in the field.

I've already discussed the myths about needing finance degrees or postgraduate education and concluded that even if you didn't have an ounce of experience in anything finance related, you could still be successful in this career. All you really need is to be prepared to learn as much as you can, as often as you can, and to find a firm with a strong support system to cover everything else.

I'm so certain of this that I'll go even further to claim that if you're one of those people who's never invested a single dollar in your entire lifetime or a person who's never looked at a portfolio outside of trying to figure out if your employer is really matching your 401(k) contribution, you, too, could become a successful planner.

How can I say this so confidently without knowing a single thing about you? Because I know that a good firm will train you; they'll teach you the things you need to know.

So why is it still the case that without even knowing exactly which skills are needed for each financial planning role, some women will just take themselves out of the running?

I can't help but hear the "I don't have the skills" argument and think what's really being said, once again, is, "I'm not a man." But I'm guessing that most women would also agree that men are not born with financial skills; they have a Y chromosome, not a $ chromosome. Besides the challenge of having to envision yourself successful in a new career that has few people who look like you in it, there's also the challenge of overcoming whatever negative thinking has been embedded in you from childhood or by societal norms in order to access the confidence to believe there's no reason you, too, couldn't do well as a planner.

The face of wealth management may still be predominantly male, so it's understandable that women would automatically exclude themselves from the pool of potential planners. But I've also noticed that there are too many women in too many fields who regularly feel like they can't be themselves in the workplace, or even feel that there's an unwritten rule encouraging them to "act like a man." There may be a whole lot of male financial planners,

As unconventional as it may sound, I truly believe that this career rewards people for having and expressing feelings.

68

but I honestly don't believe it's the case that there's any macho standard of manhood at the heart of the field. And as unconventional as it may sound, I truly believe that this career rewards people for having and expressing feelings. No one asks us to wear a poker face in the office day in and day out; quite frankly, if we did, it might actually harm our capacity to do good business. If one of your clients experiences a loss in the family, you're free to be sad and console them. If your client lands a major promotion, you can get excited for that person and maybe even celebrate with them. Wealth management doesn't require you to hide who you are. In fact, it encourages the opposite.

We've all heard the old workplace adage, "Act like a lady, but think like a man." To the contrary, in wealth management firms today, women advisors are sought after for the very reason that they don't think or act like stereotypical "men."

Spotting a Supportive Firm

Maybe you're intrigued enough to entertain the idea of pursuing a career in financial planning, but you wonder how you would find a truly woman-friendly firm, one that wouldn't let any of its associates, male or female, believe that women are not a vital addition to the wealth management field. In the prior chapter, I encouraged an open mind about websites that might be out of date in terms of not picturing the full staff of advisors within their firms. That said, you can usually spot *a really good firm* by looking at their online presence.

Beyond noticing who appears on a firm's site, read everything that you see. If you're worried about your skillset, look for information pertaining to the various types of training and support the firm offers its advisors. See if you can pick up on anything regarding the firm's culture: How do they talk about themselves? Do they pursue any charitable dealings or humanitarian efforts that may align with your own beliefs? You may have to read between the lines a little, but, if you look closely enough, the firm's culture should come through in its choices about online images and content. Check out the staff page and the company description. Click through the photo gallery, read the blog posts, and watch any uploaded videos. Ask yourself: *What's this firm's story?*

How many women are there on staff? Are all the advisors men, and do all the women work in administrative support? What's the age distribution among the people there?

A good firm will want to teach you its ways and to get you caught up on the best practices senior advisors have picked up on over the years. When a firm is willing to invest in its client-first promises, that creates fertile ground for everyone involved. When a firm mentions its mission to support advisors in obtaining their Certified Financial Planner designation, or if you've seen on the website that quite a few of the firm's advisors are already Certified Financial Planners, that's another good sign that a firm is committed to seeing you succeed.

Bear in mind that you may come across a wild card or two. There are some firms out there that are very active in the recruitment of talented women but don't go into great detail about those efforts on their websites. If you happen to come across one that does, that's a huge bonus, but smaller firms may not have enough of an internet presence to highlight their commitment to new advisors' and women advisors' success. You'll probably have to ask other people working in wealth management to name some of those firms. Or ask accountants and lawyers who work with wealth managers which firms come to their minds as potential good matches for you.

Keep in mind, too, that sometimes all of a good firm's efforts to support its employees are not obvious either from its website or from word of mouth. To find out more, you're going to have to speak with a hiring manager or an actual advisor at the company. That's an opportunity to ask about how that firm assists new hires in earning their CFP credentials, or the amount and type of in-house training offered, or whether there is a robust mentorship program already in place.

I'm sure you've received advice like this in the past: if you're curious about the field, talk to the people in it and ask them about their experiences. The more people you talk to, the better a sense you're likely to have of experiences you wouldn't otherwise know about until you lived them yourself.

I Don't Want to Be a Salesperson

The "missing skills" myth often segues into a separate but related concern. Of the skills most people fret about, selling is among the most dreaded. I've spoken with individuals who believe that the only thing financial planners do is sell life insurance, annuities, or mutual funds. Allow me to burst that bubble.

Let's start with the fact of the matter: many financial planners *do* sell products as one part of a grander scheme of services. However, it's not a requirement for all financial advisors to do this. Although it's not always a requirement, I should point out that, typically, at least within the field, women do well in the product sales area and enjoy matching clients with the best options for their needs.[16] On occasion, I've come across a woman who doesn't want anything to do with sales at all. To her, I always say, "That's perfectly OK! There are other directions for you to follow."

---

16   Daniel Vasiliu, "Men versus Women in the Sale of Financial Products," Acta Universitatis Danubius: Oeconomica 8 (2012).

Firms like Ameriprise, Edward D. Jones, Raymond James, and others may offer compensation based on product sales, but they will also offer more training to make advisors comfortable with the responsibility. As long as a product is relevant and aligns with the client's goals, most people don't have a problem with a more sales-oriented approach. Typically, advisors also have the option of working in a fee-for-service relationship with their clients, where product sales aren't that important, or don't matter at all, so you don't have to "be a salesman" of annuities, or mutual funds, or insurance policies. These firms (and their advisors) have been very successful and their clients quite satisfied.

For the companies that do place an emphasis on product sales, you'll notice that an advisor's compensation and success depends on how well they can be a "salesperson." If you definitely don't want to be a salesperson, then you shouldn't pursue an advisory job with that type of firm. But that preference absolutely doesn't mean that you should not become a financial advisor. You'll be happy to know that on the opposite side of the spectrum from sales-centric organizations are fee-only firms. Fee-only firms sell no products; they receive no compensation from brokerage firms, mutual fund companies, insurance companies, or other product providers. Their only compensation comes from fees their clients pay them.

Now you might think that the best way to avoid being a salesperson is to find work for a fee-only wealth management firm. Well, that is true, but only to a certain extent. These firms still require their advisors to perform some level of sales, just not when it comes to offering a specific product. In other words, you will still have to "sell" yourself to prospective clients. As you well know from reading earlier chapters in this book, prospects must feel that they can trust you before they will hire you. That's also true for your regular clients, insofar as they have to trust you before they'll follow through on your advice. If they can't bring themselves to do that, they're not going to pay you. Here, selling yourself—which is to say engendering trust in your capacity to do your job honestly and well—will earn you your clients' business for life. If a client has listened to your recommendations, followed through on them, and profited from that advice down the line, then not only will that client stick around for life, they'll start bragging about all you've done. In other words, they'll do the selling for you!

Ultimately, "sales" comes down to having confidence in yourself and your services and being able to project that.

A successful wealth management career will always require you to sell something, be it your products or yourself. Considering that, think about what additional questions you need to take into the interview room when you talk with firms you're interested in. If you're not keen on pushing products, then be sure to ask the recruiter how much focus the firm places on product sales and how much sales training they give their advisors. And remember, if you're good at reading people and identifying solutions to their problems, then you may want to give the whole sales thing a shot.

Wealth management success comes down to being caring and empathetic.

I've mentioned this before, but it bears repeating: wealth management success comes down to being caring and empathetic. If you can master that, everything else will flow easily and effortlessly. It doesn't matter if you find your wealth management home at an RIA firm that provides advisory services or a broker-dealer firm that sells products; it's your relationship-building skills that will make you the most valuable resource for your clients as well as for your firm.

CHAPTER 6:

"CFPs Only Work with Rich People"

YOU'RE LIKELY FAMILIAR with the saying "When the rich get richer, the poor get poorer." Income inequity may be a big social problem, but I'm always surprised when I talk with people about wealth management and some of them fold their arms across their chest to say, "I'm not into making wealthy people wealthier. I want to help the world, and I couldn't possibly do that as a financial advisor."

Of all the myths I've grown used to hearing and addressing, this one touches me the most, because I believe it stems from the most limited perspective anyone can have about managing money and investments. Contrary to popular belief, financial planning isn't about extending the gap between the "haves" and the "have nots." As a matter of fact, financial advising isn't just for the 1 percent—not at all. To the contrary, it's a field that connects its advisors with people across a broad spectrum of incomes, lifestyles, and careers.

I counter this destructive myth by pointing out that wealth management is a helping profession, one that can benefit people of all backgrounds and net worth. Financial planners make a huge impact in many different people's lives. Daily, advisors witness the differences among their clients' portfolios and work on behalf of each client to ensure that they are as prepared for their futures as possible.

If you worry that working with rich clients will benefit no one except the already wealthy, try to think about all the ways you could help those clients distribute their wealth to the less fortunate. Some of my wealthiest clients have come to me with specific desires for doing just that, but they need my help figuring out how to turn their good intentions into useful and viable resources for those in need. Whether it's education, hunger, poverty, disease—and the list is vast—the wealthiest among us are often very eager, even passionate, about improving others' lives. Just because you'll be working with people who happen to be well off doesn't mean that they've forgotten the value of doing good for others. They know they have it easier than most, and many are immensely grateful for how fortunate they've been to experience a different lifestyle. Financial advisors can make a significant difference in the world by advocating for good causes and convincing (selling!) their clients to expand their philanthropic efforts.

> *Just because you'll be working with people who happen to be well off doesn't mean that they've forgotten the value of doing good for others.*

Who among those who most wish to serve the common good wouldn't want to help the wealthy figure out how much they can afford to donate to a worthy cause? As an advisor, you can be the one who tells the client how much they need to maintain their lifestyle, how much they should keep in reserve for their kids, and how much they should gift to the causes that most need their money! Money can be used to do good in the world. Even clients who aren't multimillionaires make it their business to do their part, albeit on a smaller scale. I've had clients ranging from educators to business tycoons all looking for ways to help those who've been less fortunate.

I've discovered that pointing out the value of distributing funds to those in need is often enough of an argument to convince those skeptical of the field to give this career a shot, despite their personal feelings about capitalism. And if you're someone who believes you'd find it difficult to look beyond the massive earnings or portfolio size of high-net-worth clients, consider looking for a firm that specializes in serving a middle- to lower-income audience. Certain firms target clients who explicitly don't have a lot of money in an effort to bring financial literacy and security to underserved populations. Here's a handful of examples:

- Advisors in the Garrett Planning Network advise clients of all incomes and walks of life. Their goal is to make competent, objective financial advice accessible without any minimums as to income, assets, net worth, length of engagement, or revenues generated.

- Advisors who work for 403(b) retirement plan providers, like TIAA-CREF, work with educators, from public school kindergarten teachers to university professors.

- Advisors who work for 401(k) plan providers, like T. Rowe Price, offer one-on-one counseling sessions for all kinds of plan participants, from factory workers to department managers.

- Advisors who work for companies offering no-load mutual funds, like Fidelity, Vanguard, and Schwab, offer investment advice to a wide range of individuals trying to do the best they can with whatever amount of money they have.

- The National Association of Personal Financial Advisors (NAPFA) and the Financial Planning Association (FPA) have many advisor members who serve middle income clients' needs and who do pro bono planning for the less fortunate. The Foundation for Financial Planning has enlisted hundreds of financial planners to give free advice through programs that serve the military, those dealing with cancer, and others.

No matter where you decide to jump into the game, know that there are many different ways for you to make a difference. The financial planning profession is as much focused on giving back as it is on preserving and growing wealth. You'll have plenty of opportunity to help those in need, whether you're working with wealthy clients or those more financially strained. And now that more of the world's 1 percent have committed to making the Billionaire's Pledge, know that there's a shift happening in the way money makes the world go round. Day after day, news articles and blogs share a teaser of yet another billionaire, like Bill Gates or Jeff Bezos's ex-wife, MacKenzie Scott, who has pledged to donate most of their fortune to charity. What if you had the opportunity to help a mogul like Bill Gates figure out how to give away his portfolio and change millions of lives?

You may view them one way right now, but before long, you'll start to realize that the only thing separating the "rich" from the rest of the world is their bank accounts. Rather than view that difference as an excuse to dismiss those people in the fight for economic equality, think of them as an extension of you. With a strong relationship and lots of trust, their assets and your advice can make a significant difference in the lives of others—a difference that most of us can't always make with just our own money.

PART

2

CHAPTER 7

CFP® Certification: The Standard of Excellence

When I was an accountant, I had to work ten hours a day, seven days a week, during "tax season," which stretched from January to April, then again from September to October. I spent all those hours poring over the details of clients' tax returns, just to have half of them mad at me when they found out they owed money to the government or weren't getting as much of a refund as they'd anticipated. Some days, I struggled to find satisfaction in the job.

Becoming a CFP was a way of taking control of my career and making it my own. To me, the work involved to earn formal certification was a small price to pay for the flexibility that has followed ever since.

My shift into wealth management changed me in ways that everyone noticed, even my friends and family. Shortly after earning my CFP certification, my stress levels dropped considerably, and I was actually able to take a spring vacation for the first time. Having the freedom to make my own schedule and choose client relationships that were not likely to end in frustration and disappointment put a smile on my face that my then teenage daughter couldn't help but notice. One day, she announced at dinner, "It's like we have a whole new mom!"

In a sense, she did. Becoming a CFP created a pathway for me to be the mom I always wanted to be. It's a challenge, after all, to share the best version of yourself when you're bogged down with stressful work. Shifting my career gave me such a new lease on life that my good mood was almost contagious; everyone around me started to notice and feel the difference. My entire family reaped the benefits of that decision.

After becoming a practicing CFP, all the things about my job that once weighed me down immediately went away. No more government deadlines. No more regrettable conversations about things that were entirely out of my control. Instead, client meetings were ending on high notes, with people expressing thankfulness and relief for the time I spent working with them.

> *Earning my certification helped me make time for the things that really mattered, things I couldn't control in my previous role.*

Earning my certification helped me make time for the things that really mattered, things I couldn't control in my previous role. After earning my CFP, I was no longer one of those people who struggled to get home each day in time to have dinner with her family.

When tax time rolled around again the year after I'd become a financial planner, I had all the proof I needed. I wasn't sitting in an office drowning in W2s and 1099s and K-1s like I had been before. Instead, I was on vacation in Utah, skiing with my family.

One of the reasons I'm such a big advocate for women entering this field is because I know how much we sacrifice each and every day. I know that too often we are handed, and then take, the short end of the professional stick. After witnessing all the opportunities that were opened to me, and after noticing my own personal transformation, I can't just sit back and watch talented women settle for anything less. You deserve to be happy along with me. If you're feeling like you are "settling" for a job or career you don't want or are in an employment rut, you can change that around in this profession.

By now, I hope you've sensed that there's no one-size-fits-all approach to financial planning. This profession offers nearly two hundred different designations for advisors to choose from, ranging from focuses on retirement planning to investing to insurance. No matter what background you're coming from, you have the option to choose this career. All you have to do is want it enough to see your way through the certification process.

Get Certified

Obtaining formal certification indicates to others that you have achieved mastery of the services financial planners offer their clients.

If you happen to know anyone who's taken the exam, you've probably heard a story or two about the dedication and mental fortitude required of them as they prepared. I can assure you that the exam itself is not nearly as bad as any horror stories you may have heard—so long as you arrange to put in the study time and can practice applying what you learn along the way.

Before we talk about the specifics of test preparation, let me address why the CFP designation is so widely regarded as *the* standard of excellence in the field. The CFP Board's standards help differentiate Certified Financial Planners from others serving in the role of financial planners and advisors. What distinguishes a Certified Financial Planner from others in the role are the education, experience, and ethical obligations established and enforced by the board.

Certified Financial Planners must abide by a fiduciary standard that ensures they will always act in the best interest of the client. That may seem like a minimum requirement for any financial planner, but it's not; a financial advisor or financial planner need only recommend products or services that are *suitable*, not necessarily best, for the client. Yes, it's like that AT&T commercial where the patient is told that the surgeon getting ready to operate on him is "OK." Adding the CFP accreditation to your signature immediately lets the people you work for and with know that you take your career qualifications seriously and that you're committed to ethical excellence. Obtaining the CFP designation lets firms and clients know that you have *the knowledge and experience* to help people through some of the most important money-related decisions they will ever make. Regardless of how the financial climate may change over time, the standard set for earning the CFP designation is set by the CFP Board of Standards and updated to meet the specific issues and needs of the times.

In short, becoming a CFP lets the world know that you know your stuff and that you're capable of handling more than the rote elements of retirement planning or determining suitable insurance coverage. The education you'll receive from preparing for the CFP exam will position you to assist clients with far more than their regular investments. Earning the right to display the initials "CFP" beside your name proves that you are more than capable of delivering excellent advice.

Although the CFP designation has been around since 1972, the National Commission for Certifying Agencies first recognized the CFP certification program in April of 1995. Every few years, the program is reevaluated for compliance. According to the CFP Board CEO Kevin R. Keller, CAE: *"Given the alphabet soup of financial services industry credentials, it is vital for consumers to be able to differentiate among the various certifications and designations. Accreditation by an independent organization is a sign that the public can rely upon to determine the value of a certification since all certification programs are not created equal."* [17]

As of 2020, there were more than 89,000 Certified Financial Planner professionals in the United States.[18] According to research conducted in 2018 by the firm Cerulli Associates, 64 percent of advisors report increases in client demand for financial planning services.[19] Rising interest over the years has opened the door for even more diversity in the industry, with 2018–2019 also proving to be record years for increases in the numbers of certified women and people of color. With women still holding steady at just 23 percent of certified advisors, there's still plenty of room for improvement. Our ability to shift the scales directly relies on how well we continue to raise awareness around the potential for women to succeed in this industry.

The Four Es

Achieving certification comes from mastery of the Four Es: *Education, Examination, Experience*, and *Ethics*.

---

17   "CFP Board Achieves Milestone with 20th Year of NCCA Reaccreditation for CFP® Certification Program," CFP Board Press Release (April 1, 2015), https://www.cfp.net/news/2015/04/cfp-board-achieves-milestone-with-20th-year-of-ncca-reaccreditation-for-cfp-certification-program.

18   CFP Professional Demographics, https://www.cfp.net/knowledge/reports-and-statistics/professional-demographics.

19   CFP® Certification, "More Important in Today's World Than Ever Before" (November 30, 2020), https://www.cfp.net/knowledge/industry-insights/2020/11/cfp-certification-more-important-in-todays-world-than-ever-before.

EDUCATION

CFP professionals must demonstrate a combination of theoretical and practical knowledge of the industry. Before anyone is allowed to sit for the exam, they must complete related coursework through a CFP Board Registered Program, whether through actual college courses or through educational programs offered by institutions and private firms. Coursework covers the following:

- Professional Conduct and Regulation

- General Principles of Financial Planning

- Education Planning

- Risk Management and Insurance Planning

- Retirement Savings and Income Planning

- Estate Planning

- Financial Plan Development (Capstone) course

Certain academic degrees and professional credentials, such as CPA, Chartered Financial Analyst (CFA), or a license as an attorney may qualify a candidate for an accelerated path to certification. So CPAs and lawyers interested in this career have a big head start in the certification process.

A bachelor's degree in any discipline from any accredited college or university is also required for certification; you can satisfy this requirement prior to taking the exam or within five years of passing the test.

If you aren't fresh out of college or don't have the required coursework credits, there are plenty of ways for you to meet the educational requirements of the exam as well. Whether you're a woman working to change careers or a homemaker trying to take a new lease on life, look for registered programs that meet the CFP Board's requirements;

these can be offered by online providers or by local colleges in your area. Check the official CFP Board website for listings of approved programs and registered schools, explore those options, then decide which path will best work for you and your schedule.

EXAMINATION

Once the educational requirements are satisfied, advisors are allowed the option to sit for the exam—a test of one's ability to *apply* the knowledge they've obtained. The exam helps differentiate between advisors who can memorize and recite what they've learned from the ones who can put that knowledge into action. The test forces registrants to use their critical thinking skills in a way that most people have never been challenged to explore—even in their professional environments. That's why even seasoned advisors spend months studying in preparation.

The test is notorious for being the cause of a few sleepless nights but, overall, those who've successfully earned the right to call themselves Certified Financial Planners usually agree that those long nights were well worth it in the end.

In an attempt to keep the newest certificants abreast of relevant processes that will benefit clients, the exam is always evolving. Registrants are called on to display their proficiency in various parts of the financial planning process on top of related fields like tax planning, employee benefits, retirement plans, estate and trust law, investment management, and insurance. In March 2021, the overall pass rate for the CFP exam was 63 percent, while 67 percent of first-time test takers passed.[20]

---

20 CFP Board, "About the Exam," accessed November 11, 2021, https://www.cfp.net/become-a-cfp-professional/cfp-certification-requirements/cfp-exam-requirement/about-cfp-exam.

EXPERIENCE

Without at least a few years of relevant work experience, many advisors won't be able to pass the CFP exam at all. Relevant coursework provides knowledge of hypotheticals, but being able to apply that knowledge over the course of at least a few years of relevant work experience can be critical to earning certification.

Advisors need to complete six thousand hours (the Standard Pathway) of professional experience related to the financial planning process, or four thousand hours (the Apprenticeship Pathway) of apprenticeship that meets additional requirements. This experience must be completed within ten years before or five years after passing the CFP exam.

The *Standard Pathway* involves the following:

- Direct interaction and engagement with individual clients

- Supervision of financial planners or the financial planning process

- Direct or indirect support of the financial planner and/or the financial planning process

- Teaching financial planning–related courses at a university, offered for college credit, or at a CFP Board Registered Program

- Completing an internship or the FPA Residency Program

- *And* one or more of these:

- Analyzing and addressing client information and circumstances

- Identifying, selecting, and prioritizing client goals

- Analyzing action plans and alternatives

- Developing client recommendations

- Presenting client recommendations

- Implementing a plan with a client

- Monitoring and updating client goals and recommendations

The *Apprenticeship Pathway* involves direct interaction and engagement with individual clients completed under the direct supervision of a CFP professional, and ***all*** of the following:

- Analyzing and addressing client information and circumstances

- Identifying, selecting, and prioritizing client goals

- Analyzing action plans and alternatives

- Developing client recommendations

- Presenting client recommendations

- Implementing a plan with a client

- Monitoring and updating client goals and recommendations

ETHICS

Earning the CFP designation requires submitting to a detailed background check and staying up to date on all changes made by the CFP Board to its *Code of Ethics and Standards of Conduct*. Certificants agree to uphold strict standards of honesty and integrity and are obligated to act as a fiduciary when advising clients. CFP professionals are expected to always act in the best interest of their clients or risk being publicly sanctioned for violations.

> *CFP professionals are expected to always act in the best interest of their clients or risk being publicly sanctioned for violations.*

Different Roads to Success

In addition to reporting an amazing rate of job satisfaction, the fact that we can improve our own everyday lives while helping other people reach their goals makes the sacrifice it takes to pass the exam even more rewarding. The most appealing aspect of the profession is the way that every new advisor adds new and refreshing insights to an ongoing conversation. Since each CFP has the opportunity to travel down a different path, the combination of all our backgrounds and expertise makes for a dynamic environment.

The CFP certification process has been designed to be approached from many different angles. The way you choose to pursue the test will vary according to your experience and flexibility. I'll explain a few paths that are traveled by most people. You should feel free to choose or combine the avenues that work best for you, given your lifestyle.

Of the "Four Es," Examination and Ethics are the same no matter how you choose to work toward your CFP designation: you have to pass the exam, and you have to abide by the *Code of Ethics and Standards of Conduct*. But when it comes to the Education and Experience requirements, there are different routes you can take.

THE TRADITIONAL ROUTE

This route is taken primarily by people who identify their desire to get certified as a financial planner early on in their careers. Consider this the "path of least resistance" for high school graduates or women who've recently enrolled in a college or university. Simply choose a relevant major or pass approved courses outlined by the CFP Board and the first of the "Four Es" will already be crossed off your list.

- Education. Those who've isolated wealth management as their career of choice begin by earning an undergraduate degree that satisfies the educational requirements to sit for the exam.

- Experience. Candidates accumulate six thousand hours (about three years) of relevant experience via the *Standard Pathway*, or four thousand hours (about two years) following the *Apprenticeship Pathway*. Those who land an internship or entry-level job that meets all the Apprenticeship Pathway requirements could gain certification one year earlier than by taking the Standard Pathway.

THE ONLINE ROUTE

This route is taken primarily by those looking to change careers or reenter the workforce in a new one.

- Education. If life won't permit you to go back to school and take college courses, there are other options to complete the educational coursework requirement online. Search the web for a CFP Board Registered Program or look on cfp.net for a list. Be sure to check the course's certification to guarantee that the coursework and intermediary tests will satisfy the board's requirements. After successfully completing the coursework and passing the program's tests and exams, the online institution will certify to the CFP Board that you've met the educational coursework requirement, which will then qualify you to sit for the exam.

- Experience. You may already have met your experience requirement! If, within the five years prior to passing the exam, you worked with individual clients for at least three years in almost any financial advisory capacity, that experience could satisfy the experience requirement. If you assisted an investment broker or advisor, implementing investment recommendations, that may be good enough. If you worked with an insurance agent helping clients complete policy applications, that, too, might do it.

THE ACCELERATED ROUTE

With the board's approval, qualified applicants—those with specific academic degrees and professional credentials—can be fast-tracked to completing a *capstone course* that qualifies them to sit for the exam without needing to complete the rest of the educational coursework.

Education. The following typically qualify for accelerated approval:

- PhD in business or economics earned in the US

- Doctor of business administration earned in the US

- Licensed attorney (active/inactive)

- Licensed Certified Public Accountant (CPA)

- Chartered Financial Consultant (ChFC)

- Chartered Life Underwriter (CLU)

- Chartered Financial Analyst (CFA˚)

- CFP certification from a Financial Planning Standards Board Ltd. (FPSB) affiliate abroad

Experience. If you are working as an attorney, a CPA, an insurance or investment advisor, or as a teacher or professor with one or more of the approved degrees or credentials, chances are excellent that you've met the experience requirement. Here are some examples of what may qualify:

- Working as a CPA giving tax planning advice to clients

- Working as an attorney giving estate planning advice to clients

- Working as an insurance agent giving insurance advice to clients

- Working as an investment advisor giving investment advice to clients

To put these various options into perspective, think about it this way: every one of them requires hard work. For example, even if you pass the exam just out of college, you'll still need to fulfill the experience requirement with at least two years on the job before you can call yourself a Certified Financial Planner. And if you're someone who's already working in a closely related field, you'll still need to study to pass the exam, even if all the experience you've gained already counts toward certification. If you're someone who's not pursuing the accelerated path, I recommend that you pursue an internship or adequate on-the-job experience. Giving yourself the opportunity to see the life of a CFP in action will help you gain a better understanding of exactly what's expected of you. And if you're someone who's considering the online route, before you take that deep dive into studying for the exam, try to chart a course that gets your foot in the door at a financial planning firm, even if you start by taking advantage of an entry-level opening.

Know this too: the CFP Board has been very vocal about its desire to shorten the timeline to certification wherever possible, in an attempt to make the field more attractive to new and rising talent.

Find Your Motivation

We've had attorneys come to BRR asking what they need to do to change careers, because they were tired of trying to live up to the demand for generating billable hours. Every day, a new group of ambitious retirees, unsatisfied professionals, and hopeful college students comes to the conclusion that they want something more than what they've been accepting in their lives to date.

Of course, I'm a bit biased. But if you have a look at current surveys and reports about the field, you'll see I'm not the only person who feels so strongly about the potential associated with becoming a Certified Financial Planner. In a 2021 survey, 93 percent of CFPs rated themselves as "strongly satisfied" with their career choice.[21] In that same survey, 87 percent of CFP professionals believed they had a "competitive edge" over financial planners who aren't certified.[22] Gaining CFP certification gives people the power to present themselves in a different light, one that doesn't require them to "sell" their accomplishments as much as if they were trying to present themselves without that credential.

Imagine how good it would feel to have total professional control over the future of your career. As a CFP, you can choose whom you want to help and how you're able to help them. Certified advisors can take their personal passion and expertise and target their services to assist a specific clientele. Maybe you'd prefer to focus on high-net-worth clients. Or maybe you feel more compelled to serve clients with a much lower net worth, helping them afford to send their children to college or see a reasonable pathway to retirement. Earning your certification can give you the opportunity to offer clients whatever range of services you please. It can place your work schedule and your earnings in the palms of your hands, even allowing you the power to decide when and how you'll get paid.

---

21   CFP Board, "Survey of CFP° Professionals Shows Continued High Satisfaction with Their Career Choice, CFP° Certification," News Release (September 8, 2021), https://www.cfp.net/news/2021/09/survey-of-cfp-professionals-shows-continued-high-satisfaction.

22   Ibid.

Most planners earn compensation through one of three basic payment structures: fee-only, fee-and-commission (also called "fee-based"), and commission. To help you consider which may be best for you, here's a quick summary of what each designation means:

- <u>Fee-Only Advisors</u>: These individuals and/or firms earn hourly or flat fees, or a fee calculated on the assets they manage or the services they offer to clients.

- <u>Fee-and-Commission ("Fee-Based") Advisors</u>: These advisors charge clients an hourly, asset-based, or flat fee, then earn commissions from selling financial products.

- <u>Commission Advisors</u>: These advisors are paid based on the products their clients buy from them.

With a diverse pool of clientele and a few different options to get paid for your services, you can see that financial planning is anything but a cookie-cutter career. Every area of this profession can be determined by you, your passion, and your skills.

It's never too late to take control of your destiny. Regardless of the point from which you begin, you're going to work hard, but you can do so knowing that this career path promises some of the most satisfying long-term benefits.

CHAPTER 8:

Passing the Test

COLLEGE STUDENTS WOULD APPEAR to have it easy when it comes to qualifying to sit for the CFP exam; they only need to enroll and succeed in the appropriate coursework during their undergraduate years. However, this does not necessarily give new graduates a leg up on certification. In some instances, it may even be *harder* for college students to pass the exam compared to nontraditional applicants. More often than not, the number one thing that benefits an individual who's preparing to take the exam is having hands-on experience in financial planning. Education may be a necessary starting point, but application is what matters.

Regardless of what road you'll travel to qualify for taking the exam, I recommend placing extra emphasis on creating an action plan to prepare for test taking. Depending on your circumstances, the details of that plan may vary. From start to finish, the CFP exam demands multiple demonstrations of how proficient the applicant is *in all areas* of financial planning. It requires test takers to adopt more of a "show instead of tell" approach, solving real-world problems for fictitious clients.

We've had employees at BRR who've needed at least a year or two of experience before they felt confident enough to sit for the exam. We've had others who preferred the shotgun approach and took the exam right after graduation. Many of those in the latter group didn't pass on that first attempt, but that's easy enough to explain: most people won't know how to put together a CFP-level financial plan when they're fresh out of college. Those book smarts need to be tried and tested in the workplace before they can confidently be put into action in scenarios that run the gamut of financial concerns.

I strongly believe that the best way for a person to succeed on the CFP exam is to learn from their work experience exactly what the job entails, then use that information to develop a personalized step-by-step outline for a study regimen.

People who don't take the time to properly prepare for the exam usually find themselves heading back to the drawing board to get additional experience after the fact. It takes a lot to prepare for your first time taking the test and even more time if you'll need to take it again. My strong suggestion to you is this: don't rush to sit for the exam. In my experience, the difference between those who've passed without incident and those who came close to losing the battle was in how well they planned ahead. Practice exams go a long way toward solidifying your understanding of concepts and processes and can help to ensure that you have the skills to apply what you know to a variety of specific scenarios. I've seen too many applicants discover too late that the CFP exam isn't so much about how well you can recount the relevant material as it is about being able to prove your capacity to apply your understanding of that material in the most ethical and effective ways. That's why practice is so important.

Facing Exam Anxieties

A lot has changed since I sat for the exam. At that time, it consisted of a series of six individual tests, each covering one study area (the financial planning process, insurance, income taxes, investments, retirement planning, and estate planning). My generation also had to complete either an essay or a mock financial plan at the end of each test. The tests were only given live, three times per year, in just one or two central, proctored locations per state. You could sit for only one test on any given test date.

Today, there is one 170-question, six-hour computerized comprehensive exam from which the essay portion has been eliminated. CFP hopefuls have to answer questions that are specifically designed to challenge whether you can apply what you know to actual client situations. Some questions present mock scenarios and offer multiple-choice options that emphasize subtle complexities.

Your preparation for the exam should involve familiarizing yourself with the unique format of the questions and practicing as much as you can, as often as you can. Once you've registered with the CFP Board, you'll automatically have access to two practice exams. I highly recommend taking those, and any others you may be able to get your hands on.

Taking practice exams can help if you're someone who's vulnerable to testing anxiety or test-day jitters.

Taking practice exams can help if you're someone who's vulnerable to testing anxiety or test-day jitters. Those of you who just aren't good test takers can know the material through and through but, for whatever reason, freeze up as soon as the test officially begins. I've seen some of the best and brightest associates lose every ounce of their confidence on test day. Once panic sets in, so does forgetting all that they've studied and learned.

There was a talented CFP in our office who took the exam not once, not twice, but *three* times before she passed. I can personally attest to how well she knew the material; I saw her in action every day. She was technically gifted, and her expertise shined so brightly in her day-to-day work at the firm. For her, it wasn't the education or experience that tripped her up, it was the testing process itself.

This advisor was working for some of the best wealth managers at BRR, and she was dynamic on the job, but she just couldn't pass the exam. When it mattered most, things she knew extremely well just left her. And each time she failed, her confidence tanked even more. When the wealth managers she worked for noticed how hard she was taking her results, the team came together to help boost her confidence.

You might be surprised by how far a bit of encouragement can take a person, especially when that person is beating herself up about failing the exam. That advisor completely transformed her performance after the people she worked for banded together to support her. These were people standing in the shoes she wanted to wear, encouraging her and reminding her how smart she was. They constantly told her, "You know this!" The next time she sat for the exam, she passed. Witnessing that experience reminded me of the importance of assembling the supports you need to achieve your goals. It seems so simple an insight, but I always explicitly encourage people to develop some sort of support group while studying for the exam. Family and friends are a good place to start, but rallying other wealth management professionals to your side would make that support system even stronger.

That advisor I told you about didn't need to study any harder or longer; what she needed was to get around the psychological barriers that hindered her during the testing process. If you know that you're one of those people who can suffer from mental blocks when it's time to take a test, don't let the exam exploit those insecurities. Practice the material and find yourself a few cheerleaders to keep your spirits lifted.

Even if you aren't one of the people who struggles with test taking, please don't disregard the power of having a healthy circle of supporters as you prepare. No matter how great your intuitive test-taking skills may be, the CFP exam is such a meticulously designed test that those inherent skills aren't likely to be enough to carry you through.

Recognizing that having a support system is so important to success on the exam, the CFP Board offers a mentor program for candidates to help them connect with a dedicated CFP professional ready to help them prepare. The board is well aware that knowing how to answer the questions on the test is only part of successful preparation. And for those who would like to see how they respond to the testing environment, the board offers the opportunity to register for a formal practice exam. Registrants sit in the same type of computerized classroom with the same restrictions and resources, and with the same number of questions as on the actual exam. That's a worthwhile opportunity to work on time management and work out any test-scenario kinks that might slow you down.

Taking a formal practice test can also help registrants get a more accurate read on their strengths and weaknesses. That information can help determine where one needs more experience or to focus one's studies before the big day.

No matter how you feel about tests or how proficient you think you are in the material, take as many practice exams as you are able— whether formally or informally. I promise you'll be glad that you did.

Get Support from Your Firm

A decade ago, there were three women in our office who decided to work together to pass the test. They made a goal to earn their certification on either the first or second attempt. For added practice, they registered together for a review course. The only problem was, back then, the course they felt was best for them was offered in only one location—in a city halfway across the US. If they wanted to take that review course, not only would they have to pay to get there and back, but they'd have to miss a day or two from work. That meant using a vacation day or two, as well as spending money on flights, hotel rooms, and food.

Considering the many options that are available to registrants today, I'm able to tell you that advisors aren't required to debate whether they can afford good CFP preparation courses anymore. Although review courses may still be an added expense, those courses are offered nationwide; there's probably one right in your backyard or reasonably close to home.

I'd say a good 80 percent of the CFPs in our office invested in a review course of some sort. That percentage reflects the resources we've established to help our advisors have the best shot at passing the exam, resources that include offering reimbursement for educational and review courses as well as for exam study materials. We aren't a superlarge practice, but we've made a point of modeling our CFP support programs after some of the industry's most forward-thinking firms.

To be honest, I assume any firm would want to do everything possible to help advisors take the next steps toward earning their certification. According to the CFP Board, practices with certified professionals typically generate at least 40 percent greater revenue and are more productive than other firms. Practices known for employing CFP professionals usually attract 53 percent more high-net-worth clients than firms that don't have CFP advisors on staff.[23]

It's a win-win situation for all, so there's no reason for firms not to help their advisors take full advantage of all the resources offered for exam preparation. The board offers helpful study materials, and even offers tools and resources for supporting advisors *after* they've passed the exam.

The study group at BRR was an employee-led initiative that started with two advisors who didn't pass the exam on the first try. They decided to pair up to study for the retest, then got another associate involved along the way. One day, the group decided to develop a survey to pass around the firm, believing that it would be valuable to get some extra insight from those who had recently passed the CFP exam. With valuable survey data in hand, the group was able to create a full-scale preparation routine that helped them pass the exam together.

The key to their success, I believe, was that they were mindful to poll recent exam takers for advice. People who've had their CFP for ten or fifteen years, for example, may not offer suggestions that are particularly relevant to the current form of the test. I recommend that you pay specific attention to the recommendations from people who've passed the exam within the last two or three years. They're sure to have some good tips for you to incorporate into your study program.

Remember, too, that support needn't come in the form of a group of associates preparing for the exam as a group. It might look more like having an employer that is flexible and accommodating. It might look like access to training and mentorship opportunities

---

23   CFP Board, "Benefits of Employing CFP® Professionals," accessed November 11, 2021, https://www.cfp.net/for-employers-of-cfp-professionals/benefits-of-cfp-certification.

that are mindful of testing subject areas. It might look like the availability of company resources that can be put toward test-preparation coursework. Or, as at firms like BRR, support might take the form of financial incentives for advisors who wish to pursue the exam.

If by chance there are no clear supports or rewards built into a firm's policy or processes, that's not necessarily a reason to be deterred. It might still be possible to have your employer cover the cost of your studies. And even if the firm's budget won't allow it to foot the bill, at the very least you can ask for the opportunity to develop new skills relevant to testing subject areas. It's experience, as I've been arguing, that makes the difference between whether you pass or fail.

Try, Then Try Again

No one wants to think about failing the exam, but I need you to know that in the event that you do—as have many before—it's important to have a plan for moving forward from there.

First things first: remember that you shouldn't allow a failing result to destabilize you for too long. Don't take it personally. *The exam has a low pass rate.* Only about 60 percent of people who take it

If you don't pass the exam on the first go-around, it's important to prepare yourself for an even greater challenge on the retest.

at any given time are successful. It's not uncommon for people to fail on their first attempt. So be assured that needing to sit for the exam again should absolutely be viewed as an opportunity to keep studying and improving.

That said, if you don't pass the exam on the first go-around, it's important to prepare yourself for an even greater challenge on the retest. Yes, the test is designed to become *harder* each time you take it. But you can use the detailed exam results from each section to adjust your study plan accordingly. Measure your strengths and weaknesses, take note of where you need to shift your focus, and you'll be well set to prepare for the next attempt. I strongly urge you to take a review course or some form of practice exam that helps you in whichever areas you need to improve, especially if you skipped more formal preparation options before taking the test the first time.

In preparation for retesting, I'd also advise you to speak to your boss, or someone whose advice you trust to deliver some moral support. You'll need just as much of a support system on your second or third attempt as you need on your first.

The CFP website is a tremendous resource filled with helpful tools for becoming, and remaining, a qualified and engaged CFP. There are handbooks, practice questions, and a Candidate Preparation Toolkit; the website is an easily accessible resource for issues you might encounter from test preparation to various inflection points throughout your career. You might be surprised that one of the first pieces of advice the CFP Board offers a new registrant is the suggestion that you understand what influenced your decision to take the exam.

The board has identified categories of influence that could ultimately aid, or *hinder*, your success.

- <u>Motivation</u>: This category includes things like your role models, views, and overall expectations.

- <u>Environment</u>: This covers items like your employment, professional requirements, and access to support.

- <u>Situation</u>: This addresses items like your health, finances, and work-life balance.

- <u>Performance</u>: This section mentions your education, experience, and related skills.

Through examining each of these areas, most people are able to identify not only their inspiration for studying for the exam but the factors that could prohibit them from following through when things get challenging. If this effort on the board's part signifies anything, it's that the key to success is preparation and that applicants should be honest about how their circumstances may affect their transition to becoming a Certified Financial Planner. I think that's a helpful and realistic assessment on the part of the board: You *can* succeed; you just have to figure out where to put in the effort and how to negotiate your circumstances so that they point toward successful completion of the exam.

Use the toolkit to help you plan around any hang-ups or inconveniences—whatever may have prevented you from living up to your full potential in the past. If you're not satisfied with your work-life balance, I think that's even more of a reason to find time to study for the test.

Do you struggle with your schedule or lack an obvious support group? Check for support groups or online forums to help you reach your goals. The CFP Board has even created a Study Group Forum specifically designed for candidates preparing for the upcoming test. The Candidate Forum is another great place to network with other advisors as they prepare. These can be great places to talk through parts of the exam that may be sticking points for you.

Exam Questions

I've gathered and analyzed a few sample questions here to give you a better idea of what to expect on the actual exam.

From the CFP Practice Exam© Certified Financial Planner Board of Standards:

Sample Question #1

A young, single client approaches a CFP professional with $5,000 stating that he would like to develop a financial plan and invest in the market. This is his first experience investing and he would like help choosing an appropriate account. What is the CFP professional's most appropriate course of action?

A) *Open a brokerage account with margin*

B) *Open and fund a Roth IRA for the current year*

C) *Determine whether the client has any consumer debt*

D) *Determine whether the client has adequate life insurance*

Correct Answer: C) Of the options provided, reviewing debt is the best fit.

The CFP® professional needs additional information from the client before taking any action involving increasing client risk, such as opening a margin account. Reviewing life insurance may be appropriate for the client but does not appear to be a goal of the client. The CFP® professional does not have enough information to determine if a Roth IRA is appropriate.

Sample Question #2

Kevin earns a salary of $250,000 and an annual bonus of $300,000; he and his wife are in the 42 percent marginal tax bracket (combined federal and state). Kevin wants to contribute $100,000 toward his child's education in the next three years. Which of the following approaches minimizes his taxable gift?

A) *Paying the college directly*

B) *Contributing the funds to a Section 529 Qualified Tuition plan*

WEALTH IS WOMEN'S WORK

C) *Contributing to a Uniform Transfers to Minors Act (UTMA) account for the child*

D) *Contributing to a Coverdell Education Savings Account plan*

Correct Answer: A) Paying the school directly does not utilize any annual exclusion or credit equivalent.

Option B utilizes annual exclusions and possibly credit equivalent unless Kevin's wife agrees to gift split, and option C uses both annual exclusion and credit equivalent, even with gift splitting. Regarding option D, Kevin is not eligible due to income.

Sample Question #3

A CFP® professional meets with two new clients who would like advice about their mortgage. In the review, the CFP® professional finds that their essential expenses exceed their income. Mortgage rates have come down significantly and they intend to refinance their current 30-year mortgage to a 15-year mortgage. Their payments will be higher than their current payment. However, they will pay off the mortgage five years earlier than the current amortization schedule allows. What should the CFP® professional do?

A) *Suggest they stay with their current mortgage, as the higher interest is tax deductible*

B) *Suggest they refinance to a 30-year fixed mortgage and begin funding savings*

C) *Suggest they refinance to the 15-year mortgage, which would reduce the amount of interest paid over the life of the loan*

D) *Suggest they meet with their mortgage broker*

Correct Answer: B) The clients have a negative cash flow and should reduce their payments as much as possible and establish a cash reserve.

This brief overview of the kinds of questions you can expect on the test should give you a sense of why it's important to work through as many practice questions as you can and take practice exams and even a review course if you are able. Ideally, you'll develop the ability to explain in your own words the reasoning behind the correct answers. When you can't, that's a sign that you likely need to place more focus on that particular area of study as you prepare to sit the exam.

CHAPTER 9:

The Power of Internships

AARON FIRST CAME TO WORK for us as an intern over fifteen years ago. There were a few interns working at BRR that summer, and our plan was to offer one of them work as a full-time assistant financial planner. Aaron was the best prospect within the group. He had impressed us with his intelligence, drive, and work ethic, and we could see him becoming a valuable employee. But he hadn't graduated from college yet and couldn't really work full time while he was completing his college courses. The new hire had to have a college degree and commit to a full-time schedule, so we found ourselves offering the job to one of the other interns instead. But we didn't want to lose Aaron, so we created a new job that was half intern and half administrator and asked him to stay on in that position until he graduated. Even though the timing wasn't quite right after he interned that summer, we saw a lot of potential in him and created the right circumstances for keeping him on. We wanted to be sure to invest in him so that we could hire him on full time once he completed his degree. He graduated, and we hired him as an assistant financial planner.

Aaron was never afraid of taking the initiative to learn more, even when that meant silently observing the way senior advisors dealt with clients. He became a CFP a couple of years later, then was promoted to associate financial planner and to financial planner. A few years after that, one of our senior planners left the company. Given the emphasis on client relationships, whenever there is turnover among senior planners, a company risks losing those clients who worked closely with that person. Our senior planner's clients had built strong relationships with him over the years, and so we knew this was a sensitive situation that needed to be handled delicately.

After surveying our personnel, we decided to promote Aaron to senior financial planner and give him responsibility for these clients. Despite having no personal connection with any of them, he did a remarkable job of gaining their trust. We didn't lose a single client during that transition. As a matter of fact, not only did Aaron excel with clients and in supervising and managing an assistant financial planner, his team eventually grew. In time, we gave him responsibility for even more clients, and we added two more people for him to manage.

In 2013, my former partner, Jim Budros, wanted to sell his shares in the firm, and we decided it was time to share ownership with a few key employees. Before then, we never had a minority shareholder at BRR, so we spent a lot of time contemplating whom we could trust. We decided to choose four employees to split those shares, and Aaron happened to be one of them. Continuing his climb up the ladder, the shareholders nominated him to be a member of the board of directors, and to this day, he still sits on our board. Aaron also leads our ultra-high-net-worth team. He has five people working for him and is managing a group of very valuable clients for the firm.

Aaron's case is unique insofar as he went from a summer internship to a part owner and board member of our firm. But it's not *so* unique that it couldn't happen again.

Fast-forward fifteen years. Michaela was a junior in college majoring in finance when she became the very first winner of our Peggy M. Ruhlin Women in Wealth Management Scholarship. After winning the scholarship, she was offered a paid internship at our office for the summer. From day one, she was never shy about taking advantage of any and every opportunity to learn. Not only did she choose an educational course load that automatically satisfied the CFP Board's requirements, but during her internship, she didn't wait for opportunities to come to her. Instead, she created opportunities for learning by asking questions and generally trying to absorb as much as she could.

She did such an outstanding job working with us that, by the time the internship ended, our firm had already extended her an employment offer. Michaela trained and worked with us for another year or so before registering to take the CFP and passing the exam with flying colors. She's been promoted twice, and she's even chaired the firm's scholarship committee!

> *It is possible to transition seamlessly from undergraduate internship to job offer to CFP credentialing and beyond.*

Michaela's story, like Aaron's, shows that it is possible to transition seamlessly from undergraduate internship to job offer to CFP credentialing and beyond. And Michaela, like Aaron, seems to me someone who is one day likely to find herself a shareholder or partner of a successful firm (hopefully ours).

Who Should Pursue an Internship?

If you're still in school, an internship is the easiest way to get to know more about a firm you're interested in working with; it's a great way to help that firm get to know more about you too. Of course, it can also be a fantastic opportunity to jump-start your on-the-job experience and gain exposure to real-life financial planning.

Each year, more college students are being introduced to the benefits of a career in wealth management at their school's job fairs and other hiring events. BRR, for example, is a very intern-friendly firm, because we've recognized the value of hiring from within. Not only are we willing to help you build your career skills, but we'll offer all the support you need to get there.

That means we're traveling to campuses for outreach programs, trying to find current students who may have an interest in the field and be a good fit for our team. But here's the thing: when I talk with young women planning to work in finance, I'll learn that they're all looking at careers as financial analysts making judgments about competing stocks and their trajectories. You can imagine by now that I do my best to share with them the ways that a career in wealth management provides the opportunity to do financial analysis, plus so much more.

When I present them with the option to have some form of contact with the general public and avoid sitting at a desk all day, staring at their computer screens, many see that a career as a financial planner could make them happier, while allowing them to do something that also interests them.

Given that we know the value of engaging interns, at BRR we do everything we can to ensure that there's interesting work and useful learning taking place among those we invite onto our staff. We've hired employees who've come to us after interning in another job, either feeling that another firm was not a good fit for them or having grown bored from cold-calling a list of numbers all day. My advice to you is to learn what you can about the sorts of experiences you'll be offered as an intern at a particular firm. Spending eight hours a day attempting to set up appointments for the financial planner you're working for isn't the best introduction to the job. BRR does our best to highlight how fulfilling our relationships with clients can be. Our interns love the idea of doing something they're good at and helping people in the process. Of course, there's always some degree of administrative work, but we fully realize that it's not the administrative tasks that are going to convince young and bright minds that a career in wealth management is attractive. So we allow our interns to take on as much as they want and actually encourage them to explore more aspects of the job than what they find they're comfortable doing.

An intern at our firm can ask to sit in on client meetings, participate in investment reviews, and otherwise get experience doing just about anything they're legally allowed to do in the role. But, as I pointed out earlier, getting to do those things also requires that interns make the most of the opportunity and not be intimidated by what they don't yet know.

We want our interns to get a true feel of what this industry can offer. We let every intern know that the internship will become only what they make of it. We give them a list of things that we encourage them to do and experiences we want them to have, but we won't force them along.

Now, say you're unable to land an internship at a wealth management firm like BRR. There are still plenty of options available to you. There are lots of financial advisory or financial services firms that may give you a taste of the wealth management experience. Of course, they may not give you a full-scale introduction into the breadth of the wealth management services spectrum, but that experience will be valuable as you make your way forward, nonetheless. In my opinion, any opportunity you can find that will allow you to see financial planning in action is worth pursuit.

Elya John was the 2021 winner of the Peggy M. Ruhlin Women in Wealth Management Scholarship, and she went on to win one of twelve $10,000 Charles Schwab RIA Talent Advantage® Student Scholarships. In the essay she submitted as part of her scholarship application, Elya said, "It was not until I shadowed an investment advisor that I realized the impact my career could have on others, and after this, I knew I was on the right track."

She went on to say, "Some of the most impactful leaders I have met through college and internships have been women. They bring diverse perspectives to this industry that will help shape the future of financial planning."

Gaining valuable experience can help you on your path to becoming a CFP no matter where you're working, and once you pass the exam, you'll instantly become a much more attractive candidate to your dream firm should you have one. And internship hours count toward the CFP experience requirement!

If you're in a situation that won't allow you to take on an internship, then I would suggest taking a job in a financial planning firm that may not pay as much as the job you're currently working. There are many firms that are willing to take a chance on you, knowing that all you have to do is pass the exam. In many cases, finding a potential employee who's interested in the CFP, no matter what level position they're interviewing for, is a welcome thing for a firm.

Whatever type of opportunity you select, be sure to use that introduction to firm life to do some networking. Make yourself an invaluable addition to the office, no matter if you're working in finance, accounting, or even law. Discuss your goals with people you trust. If the job offers exposure to other women who are financial planners, or working for financial planners within the firm, talk with them about their work and let them get to know you. Find out what they did to make it to where they are in their career and, when the opportunity presents itself, find out how you can expose yourself to similar opportunities.

> *Whatever type of opportunity you select, be sure to use that introduction to firm life to do some networking.*

Like any other business, financial planning has networks that, when properly leveraged, could help you see your options and move your career forward.

Internship Checklist

I love a good checklist, and I'd be remiss if I didn't point out how important it is to create a goal sheet for your internship, to make sure you get the most out of the experience. Here are a few suggestions to get you started.

- ☐ *Write down your goals.* What do you want to get out of the internship? Are you looking to embellish your resume? Would you like an employment offer from the firm?

- ☐ *Write down your questions.* Before accepting the internship, get a feel for what you'll be doing. Ask about the average day of an intern. Ask questions to determine what's encouraged and what's restricted. See who you'll be working for and make sure their job description will place you in a position to learn.

❐ *Outline an action plan.* Know how you'll proceed through the internship months to maximize your chances of gaining experience in different subject areas.

❐ *Write down your interests as they develop.* What aspect of financial planning are you most enthusiastic about? Investments? Retirement planning? If you aren't really sure where your interests lie, how can you use this internship to learn more and get closer to identifying them?

Remember, an internship can yield valuable experience when it comes to seeking employment and eventually working toward the CFP designation. Make the most of the opportunities presented to you and the people you're there to learn from.

CHAPTER 10:

The Law of Attraction

RECENTLY, I BECAME AWARE of a New Age phenomenon known as the Law of Attraction, which encourages people to "think" their way to success by being positive, staying focused, and visualizing their goals.

I do think it's a good idea to remain positive, especially when you're taking on a challenging task. I also think it's wonderful to have a clear vision of where you want to go. However, if you truly want to be successful, in any capacity, all the thinking and visualization in the world won't help you until you decide to put some action behind it.

The same applies to how far you'll advance in your career as a financial planner; there's nothing that can solidify your ability to succeed except hard work and dedication. That's what you should be focused on from day one as any firm's newly hired associate.

When you first start a job with a financial advisory firm, you will almost never be expected to bring in clients for yourself or the firm. Instead, you'll work under the supervision of an experienced advisor who is doing the work of finding and signing new clients.

Eventually, you'll have to do some client prospecting and business development on your own. You'll remember from an earlier chapter that even if you won't be expected to sell products or obtain new clients, you'll be responsible for "selling yourself," so to speak. Clients have to pick up on your knowledge and confidence every time you speak with them.

All that's to say: the only Law of Attraction that I want you to focus on is how you're going to position yourself to attract great clients. Your firm may work as a team but, essentially, every advisor in that office will also operate as an independent entity. If you've ever been to any sort of sales or marketing event, you've probably heard a speaker say, "Move as if you're the CEO of your own business." That really is the key to building a successful wealth management career.

> *It takes effort to attract clients and even more work to get them to stick around.*

It takes effort to attract clients and even more work to get them to stick around.

Bring the Passion

Introverts can become paralyzed by the thought of socializing with complete strangers, even if they're great at building and sustaining relationships. Financial planning is an interpersonal industry, so if you're aware of your own tendencies to introverted behavior, I want to encourage you to learn how to play the part.

Years ago, everyone in our firm took the Myers-Briggs Type Indicator personality inventory. Contrary to our expectations, of the twenty-five or so people we had working for us at the time, only three registered as extroverts on the survey! That's to say: we've had plenty of introverted advisors work for our firm who have learned to make the more extroverted-seeming requirements of the job work for them.

Those who have some anxiety around meeting new people have found ways to partner with others. If you're able to form a group with fellow advisors in your firm, you'll eventually discover the one or two people who are much more comfortable doing the talking. Let the extrovert in the group be the one who's up on the stage, leading the presentation and running the show. Then watch and learn from that person whichever habits of theirs you most want to emulate.

Others have found models and mentors who share their same personality characteristics and learn from them techniques for doing well in this career. Likewise, you might look for like-minded people in your firm with whom you can work comfortably, no matter their personality type.

I happen to be an extrovert, but that doesn't mean I haven't had to develop and practice my social and selling skills. One of the things that has helped me broaden my reach and put myself out there was taking the time to practice my response to that perennial question everyone gets asked: *What do you do?*

It's important to have a good answer to that inquiry. I'm not talking so much about a technically detailed answer as I am about a personal answer—a description that lets people know that you love what you do and makes them remember your enthusiasm after the conversation ends.

Think about how many people talk about their careers during casual conversation, then think about how many times you've truly remembered their answers. When someone offers me the basic two-step elevator pitch, I'm probably not going to be moved enough to hold on to that information. Most people tend to tune out— either because we've learned not to expect an interesting answer to the question or because some people offer job descriptions that end up sounding like a hard sales pitch. Awkward moments can arise from underselling one's strengths, but more times than not, they arise because people give the answers they *think* others want to hear rather than speak more authentically about their interests and motivations.

When you're clear about your passion, others will be interested.

My way of responding to questions like "What do you do?" is something like, "I work for the greatest firm, Budros, Ruhlin, & Roe. I just love it! We're a wealth management firm that ..." Then I'll make note of a couple of the specific things we do for our clients. If the opportunity arises naturally, I might also offer an example of something I just did to help a client: "Just today, I helped a grandmother set up 529 college savings plans for her four grandchildren. She is just thrilled to be able to do that!" For me, the details of the job aren't as important as it is to make sure I express my enthusiasm for what I do. When people can tell how much you love your work, they're more likely to want to hear more.

You don't have to be a salesperson to express your feelings in a convincing way. Tell people why you enjoy what you do and, trust me, they'll remember what you said. They may even become interested in having a more in-depth conversation or becoming a client. When you speak about what makes your job meaningful, not only do you remove the feeling that you might be "selling" something, but you'll also potentially open up opportunities for sharing information, exchanging business cards, or otherwise inviting future contact.

It's also the case that many firms have a "closer" or someone in business development whose primary task is to step in and partner with you in the process of working with prospective clients. In our firm, that's Gary. When an advisor comes across a person who's interested in our services, Gary is the go-to guy for making sure the interaction moves in a positive direction. Find the Gary of your office if you know you have trouble sealing the deal and work closely alongside that person in moments when you sense you've made contact with a potential client.

Remember, financial planning is about building relationships, and that includes taking advantage of opportunities within your network to put yourself out there and talk with people about their interests.

Build Your Community

If you have some anxiety around the thought of being responsible for attracting new clients, it can help to think about all the things you do throughout the day and all the spaces in which you're naturally comfortable.

What type of activities do you participate in? What organizations and businesses do you frequent?

In any given week, you might visit a school, a library, a place of worship, a restaurant. All of these are opportunities for you to gain exposure for your wealth management skills and practice your passion pitch. When you're looking to build up your clientele, start with your own community. You'd be surprised who you meet just by talking to your friends, family, and colleagues.

You'd also be surprised what you learn. Don't assume that you know everything there is to know about your inner circle. Your best friend may have a wealthy great-aunt that she never talks about. Your child's coach may eventually inherit some money and need help deciding what to do. We've had people in the office join a Rotary Club to build their networks. Others have volunteered with charitable organizations or taken positions on various boards of directors—each of these activities puts you in touch with new people. If you're new to financial planning, you aren't going to get on the board of the United Way, but that doesn't mean there isn't a nice start-up or a small charity that's struggling and in need of some help. Check out the PTO board at your child's school or maybe even the local chapter of the Scouts. And join the Financial Planning Association and attend the local chapter's meetings. Those will be full of like-minded people who can share ideas and experiences.

Most of all, don't look for immediate opportunity when you're having these conversations; look at your engagement with various groups in your community as a time to solidify *your position* as *the* financial planner on whom people can rely. There are whole groups of people out there waiting on your expertise; you just have to put forth the initiative to find them.

Let People Get to Know You

People need the opportunity to get to know you and to have some understanding of who you are and what you do. When you regularly plant that seed throughout your community, others will start to make connections for you. When someone asks your neighbor, fellow board member, or the principal of your child's school a question about wealth management, that person should be in a position to say, "Oh, you need to talk to Sharon; she's a financial planner." Your name and wealth management should become synonymous. If people know who you are and what you do, you're more likely to become the first person who comes to mind when they need to make a referral. I can't tell you how many times

The relationships you have with the people in your community will eventually open new doors.

a new client has told me that so-and-so referred them to me, and I don't know who so-and-so is, but I come to find out that so-and-so's brother is on a board with me. The relationships you have with the people in your community will eventually open new doors.

This is why I always stress the importance of getting out there and making your presence known. Don't look at those everyday interactions as one-off conversations. There's opportunity in every encounter. Word of mouth is the best form of advertising, and people can't talk about you if they don't know you. Put in the work to make yourself known and make known that you know your stuff.

A lot of people turn to social media to advertise their business. It's free and fast, and it potentially connects you with millions of people. That said, whether or not it can be useful to you depends on your target demographic. In 2022, for example, you won't find a lot of retirees scrolling for wealth management professionals on Instagram. Think about your client base and areas of expertise before investing in your social media presence as a way to attract clients. Think, too, about the overall message of this book: it's one thing to be an online presence, another to use online alternatives to establish yourself as an authority in your field, still another to establish personal relationships with the people around you.

Depending on the firm you work for, there may also be someone, or a team of people, whose job it is to promote the business through social media. BRR has a whole marketing initiative focused solely on social media. We even have a separate website for our younger audiences and a whole team dedicated to catering to that demographic. We work to remain sensitive to generational group habits, as well. In recent years, for example, we've recognized an entirely different breed of investor that comes from the millennial generation: people who work for years in well-paying jobs long before they buy homes, get married, or have children. Our firm recognized the importance of attracting this new category of client early on to make sure they get the longer-term help best suited to their specific needs.

We've made it part of our mission to help young, successful people develop knowledge and good habits so they won't fall prey to unreliable investment opportunities and so that they can live the futures they envision for themselves. By hosting seminars and meeting younger clients where they are, we've been able to identify and help a whole new generation of people who need our help.

Whether in your firm or in your community, don't be a shadow on the wall. If you want to be the go-to person, whether among your colleagues, clients, or community, then let them see how much you've invested into building your own brand. They have to trust that whenever they're in need, you're the person who can help them. Whether your center of influence is outside the firm or within the firm, it's the same principle. Get creative and be aware of everyday opportunities to share what you do and what you know. When you're always representing your best self and your business acumen, you'll never have to "sell" a thing.

CONCLUSION:

To My Fellow CPAs

I'M NO LONGER a practicing CPA, but I remember those days quite vividly—especially between January and April of each year. It's hard for nonaccountants to understand how stressful, how mind-numbing, how soul-destroying tax season can be, and I believe it takes a much larger toll on women practitioners who still shoulder the majority of family care.

Over the past few weeks, I've been following #taxtwitter (on Twitter, of course), and it's painful to read the posts from tax preparers lamenting their long workdays and seven-day workweeks, as well as the lack of cooperation or gratitude from their clients. I haven't prepared a tax return for money in thirty-four years, but it seems like *nothing* has changed; in fact, things might be even worse.

Please think about a new career in wealth management. You are so prepared to be a successful financial advisor: you can solve problems, you know how to communicate with clients, you're not afraid of number crunching.

This profession is waiting for you, waiting to give you enormous job satisfaction, financial reward, work-life balance and much, much less stress! Hardly a day goes by, especially during tax season, that I don't thank my lucky stars that I found my way here.

To My Industry Colleagues

IF YOU'RE READING THIS BOOK because you're a woman interested in a wealth management career, what I have to say here can help you determine which firms might be a good fit for you. If you're reading this chapter or this book because you're a firm owner, executive, manager, or senior advisor, I want to remind you of the good reasons to ensure that your firm supports women advisors at all levels and encourage you to adopt and expand practices that invite more women into your company.

You've likely heard or read about all the benefits of inviting more women advisors into your firm. You understand that having talented women representing your business is a good business practice. As the owner of a successful firm, I can say with confidence that there are bottom-line rewards for making concerted efforts in this direction. If you want your company to be more successful, all signs indicate that you need to hire more women. Consider just these two: firms with more women CFPs will be more likely to attract and retain baby boomer women clients, who are expected to control more assets as they outlive their spouses; and firms with more women CFPs are less likely to miss out on opportunities to serve millennial women clients, a group that is overall less likely to share financial responsibility with—or hand it over to—spouses.[24]

I recognize that many firms have already adjusted their business plans to try to increase the number of women in their workforce to at least 25 percent. But I want to walk you through a few ways that you can work toward making your business more attractive to new talent.

Create the Demand

First things first: get the word out. Let more women know about the advantages of this career. Be truthful about what women can expect when they join your firm, and highlight whatever programs you offer to benefit them specifically.

When I first spoke at the Women in Economics Club at Ohio State University, almost 80 percent of the women in the audience had never heard of wealth management. Of the small percentage who knew what it was, very few considered it a potential career choice. And this group was one of the best pools of talent any firm could dream of choosing from!

These were women with a strong interest in finance and economics. Yet, in their view, their only career paths were investment banking, stock analysis, and the like. Whatever they'd heard about wealth management was peppered with misconceptions. Some thought it was a modern-day adaptation of old-school stock brokering. They didn't realize there was a planning component to the work. And they certainly

---

24   Sophie Schmitt, "Building a Diverse Practice: CFP® Certification to the Female Value of Advisors" (April 2021), © 2021 Aite Group LLC, https://www.cfp.net/-/media/files/cfp-board/knowledge/ Reports-and-Research/Aite-Research/CFP-Board-Building-a-Diverse-Practice-The-Value-of- CFP-Certification-to-Female-Advisors-Report.pdf.

had never considered the relational aspect of the job. Talking with groups like these helps change the perception of some and present a more accurate description of the work for the rest. Similarly, when I've pointed out the ways that this work has a strong service component— helping people reach their goals—I've felt a palpable change in the audience's demeanor and interest. By debunking various myths and offering a more detailed and nuanced account of the field, we're contributing to shifting the narrative for future conversation those women might have with other women like them.

I strongly recommend to other wealth management firms that you think about how to spread the word about why women need to choose to work for you.

I strongly recommend to other wealth management firms that you think about how to spread the word about why women need to choose to work for you. Take a trip to local colleges and universities in your area. Visit wealth management groups in your area, or if none exist, start one and invite interested women to attend your meetings. Consider making presentations to high school students to encourage their interest. You might even create a primer course or scholarship program that triggers interest among high school seniors, so they go into college with the intention of preparing for a wealth management career.

Our firm had been offering paid internships for years when we finally decided to create a scholarship opportunity specific to young women. Prior to the year we established the scholarship, we went through several seasons during which there were no women applicants at all for our internship posts. In a typical year, we have seventy-five applications for internships, with only about 25 percent of those from women. Then one of our female assistant wealth managers suggested that we create a specific incentive just for women—what would become our now well-established Peggy M. Ruhlin Women in Wealth Management Scholarship. For the scholarship's inaugural year, we concentrated our attention on applicants in Ohio, since they would be most likely to take a job offer with us.

That program helps us get the word out and offers monetary incentive for women to learn about a field we hope they'll grow to love. In most years, we come across multiple applicants who come close to winning the scholarship, and so we typically offer one or two of them a paid summer internship as well. Incentivizing our target audience after identifying our market means that now we never struggle to get talented women through our office door.

Recruit Professionals

Experienced career women with transferable skills are the next group we need to ensure knows about the options in the wealth management profession. Lawyers, accountants, and bankers are all examples of women whose training would make for an easy transition to wealth management. And be sure not to exclude women with all their professional credentials who may have taken an indefinite leave from their prior jobs. Find the women's groups in your area that may attract already well-credentialed women who may be underemployed or otherwise unhappy with their current careers. As someone who made a midcareer decision to switch fields, I always make it a point to seek out women who may be as frustrated with their current employment as I once was.

Your firm could decide to host an open house and invite women accountants and attorneys to talk about what wealth managers do. You'd be surprised how many women will show up for a heart-to-heart with fellow female professionals—whether for networking or mutual support, and, of course, because of curiosity and interest in the job and the career satisfactions it offers.

And if you're looking for an easy way to begin recruiting more women, the CFP Board is a great resource. Through its Center for Financial Planning, you can take advantage of the Financial Planner Re-Entry Initiative, which is designed specifically to promote pathways for professional women interested in pursuing a wealth management career.

Look within the Industry

Not all recruiting efforts need to start from square one. There are women across the wealth management industry who could benefit from working with a firm that recognizes the added value of having women advisors. Some firms aren't yet successful at helping their women advisors reach their full potential. If you're running a company that's assembled the necessary resources to aid women in their journey to provide clients with the best possible service, then you're ready to attract advisors who will likely be better off working for you.

Check your local chapter of the Financial Planning Association (FPA) to locate women in the industry. Then consider starting a blog or study group specifically for women and use it as a platform for discussing all kinds of issues surrounding wealth management. If you want to tailor the discussion even more, you could focus on topics that are specifically centered on women or start conversations that may concern women more than men. Through these efforts, you'll establish a new pool of potential employees.

Don't forget to look within your own firm too. Maybe there is a woman working in administration or data management who would eagerly accept some mentoring toward becoming an advisor; make it known that you have opportunities to train internal talent to further their careers.

Look the Part

Is your firm an attractive destination for women planners? If so, in what sense? Could a woman interested in your firm look at your website and see that she would be welcome there? Do you host interesting groups, seminars, and outreach programs? Does your staff page indicate that you have successful teams of women advisors? Do the images featured across your site feature women planners as frequently as men? Are any claims of diversity and support for women supported or contradicted by those images? Imagine potential women advisors looking at a firm website that shows the following: all the senior and executive roles are filled by men, and all the firm's administrative roles are filled by attractive young women. What impression is that likely to give?

If you do have plenty of women advisors to showcase, be sure that's reflected in your web presence. Then consider taking things a step further. At BRR, for example, we've created a series of web pages specifically tailored to both women clients and women employees. We utilize those pages to talk about the benefits of a career in financial planning, and we've included insights and testimonials from women who work as advisors in our office. Including a group photo of all the women advisors at our firm sends a positive message to women who are looking for their "place" in wealth management and to women looking for a wealth management firm that is highly likely to value them as clients.

We've done a great deal to make sure that our presence online and elsewhere reflects our mission. We want anyone who searches for Budros, Ruhlin & Roe or makes contact with us in whatever format to know that we are more than just one of the best firms in the country; we want it to be unquestionably clear that our company is very women-friendly and that any woman interested in doing business with us would fit right in.

We've even turned our efforts to support women into a community all its own. Our women advisors work together on local service projects. We make the idea of working for us or hiring us to manage investments feel much more personal. We want there to be no question that we care.

Offer Attractive Compensation

Painting an attractive picture will carry your firm only so far; so be sure to offer the right pay, benefits, and working conditions.

The issue of equal compensation should go without saying. You shouldn't pay women less than men for doing the same job when they have the same experience. Your pay has to be competitive if you want to attract the best talent. If you own a firm, you already know that.

What you may not realize is how important it is for women to receive great benefits that acknowledge and accommodate their unique needs. One of the main concerns for professional women is having the ability to utilize flextime in setting their office schedules. If they have children, for example, they may have to get kids onto the bus in the morning or drive them to day care, and so they may need to start their workday a little later than others. Oppositely, they might have great childcare arrangements in the early part of the day but will need to begin work earlier so that they can leave a little earlier in the afternoons.

The COVID-19 pandemic has taken "flextime"—work from home vs. work in the office—to a whole new level. As so many firms had to switch to this new way of doing business, they found that employees working from home could be just as productive, and that they didn't need to work a standard "9 to 5" workday to be that productive. So flextime in a pandemic-free world should be a no-brainer.

Of course, you likely already recognize that it's good for both the men and women in your office for you to have a solid maternity/parental leave policy, as well as adequate paid time off for illness, including time spent in a caregiving role.

Then you might offer other perks. Since the day our firm was founded, we've had a "Friday afternoons off" policy. If an employee does not have a critical need to get something done before the weekend, they can work just five and a half hours on Friday. So if they start work at 8:00 a.m., they can go home at 1:30 p.m. That means employees know that they can schedule doctors' and dentists' appointments on Friday afternoons, or just let their family look forward to some extra time with them then. We are also committed to closing the office between the Christmas and New Year's Day holidays each year, and to do so by giving every employee an extra week of paid vacation / family time. If you care about work-life balance, find ways of proving that through both formal and informal employee policies.

> *If you care about work-life balance, find ways of proving that through both formal and informal employee policies.*

Offer Resources and Support

Pay attention to the dynamics in your office and develop supports that meet the specific needs of your employees. Our firm has a study group that is just for our women employees. We meet once a quarter at the office to have lunch, catch up, and learn something together. Sometimes we'll watch and respond to a TED Talk; other times we'll discuss a pertinent book we've all read. My initial goal when I started those sessions was to help the women in our office develop greater confidence. I wanted them to form relationships with one another in order to feel more empowered when it was time to contribute to office-wide discussions. Before we started the group, our women advisors would rarely be the first ones to volunteer information at company meetings, even though I knew they had great insights to share. Shying away from the spotlight was, for some, an ingrained habit, so I wanted to create a forum that might have the effect of making them feel more comfortable speaking up and speaking their minds.

The confidence developed within the group had effects that exceeded their interaction with others in the firm. They were also able to translate tips and information we developed in our group sessions in conversations with their clients, their friends, and all kinds of other people they came in contact with. You can be sure that once we noticed the positive results, we made sure to post group updates on our company website so visitors could see how dedicated we were to seeing women succeed.

Specific and responsive action—that's the best support you can give. Use your firm's leverage to help women adapt to an industry that is still dominated by men.

When you think of "resources and support," I would also encourage you to think about ways that your firm can invest *finan-*

cially in the women who work for you. I've already mentioned the scholarship and paid internships at BRR, but we also provide financial resources to help our advisors *throughout the life cycle of employment with us.*

For example, we pay for all of our advisors to be members of the Financial Planning Association and the National Association of Personal Financial Advisors (NAPFA). We also find local membership organizations that offer valuable networks and opportunities, like a group here in Columbus called Women for Economic and Leadership Development (WELD). We encourage our women advisors to attend WELD's monthly meetings and seminars and pay the fees for anyone who wants to participate. We cover the costs of participating in other groups, events, and fundraisers that celebrate women in business, women in finance, and women in leadership. Our focus is not just on how we can help women succeed but on how we can help them become leaders within this profession.

For us, that means including men alongside the women, especially when it comes to sponsorship of events. For woman-centric events—a WELD event, for example—that our firm chooses to sponsor, we'll be sure that our table has both men and women representing the firm and talking with attendees. By sending some men to help express our interest in helping women succeed, we can be even more convincing that we're serious about that part of our mission. We're showing audiences that the women are not doing one set of activities or thinking one way and the men another. They share responsibilities and work together toward their joint success and toward building our firm's standing in the field.

Acknowledgments

WRITING THIS BOOK helped fulfill my passion for introducing more women to the career that has been so fulfilling to me—intellectually, emotionally, and financially. I want to acknowledge the women whose guidance, support, and friendship I treasure:

Alexandra Armstrong, CFP®, my role model. She was the first female president of the International Association for Financial Planning, and ten years later, I was the second.

Andrea Ellis, CFP®, Samantha Anderson, CFP®, Jamie Rizer, CFP®, Jessica Lee, Sonia Brinkman, and Michaela Loveday, CFP® (first winner of the Peggy M. Ruhlin Women in Wealth Management Scholarship), who inspired me every day at work.

My "gourmet girls" Donna, Jan, and Patti. I treasure our friendship.

My sister, Nancy Miller Kelly, and my daughter, Megan Ruhlin Kolb, for whose love and support I am grateful every day; and my mother, Shirlee Miller, who I miss every day.

About the Author

PEGGY RUHLIN, CFP®, CPA/PFS (Retired)

Peggy Ruhlin is the retired Chair of the Board of Directors of Budros, Ruhlin & Roe. She was formerly its Chief Executive Officer (2000–2019). Peggy has been recognized as one of America's most distinguished women in wealth management: recipient of the 2017 Alexandra Armstrong Award for lifetime achievement, named one of the "20 Most Influential Women to Watch in 2016" by *Investment-News*, one of the Top 25 Women RIAs in 2016 by WealthManagement.com, and one of the *Financial Times* Top 100 Women Advisers in 2014.

Under Peggy's leadership, Budros, Ruhlin & Roe won the 2011 Schwab Impact Awards® Best in Business award.

She has served on the Board of Directors of the Certified Financial Planner Board of Standards, Inc., the Schwab Advisor Services Advisory Board, and as a trustee of the Washington, DC-based Foundation for Financial Planning. She was also president of the International Association for Financial Planning and was instrumental in the formation of the Financial Planning Association.

Peggy is a trustee emerita of Otterbein University, having previously served as a trustee (2001–2014), vice-chair of the Board of Trustees, and chair of the Investment Committee. She was a commencement speaker at Otterbein's 2022 graduation ceremony, at which she received an honorary Doctor of Humane Letters degree.

Contact

You can reach Peggy at Peggy.Ruhlin@b-r-r.com, or connect with her on social media:

Twitter: http://twitter.com/peggyruhlin

LinkedIn: http://linkedin.com/in/peggyruhlin